At Your Service

By the Junior League of Gwinnett and North Fulton Counties

At Your Service

Southern Recipes, Places and Traditions

This cookbook is a collection of favorite recipes,
which are not necessarily original recipes.
Published by the Junior League of Gwinnett
and North Fulton Counties, Inc.

Library of Congress Catalog Number: 2001130431
ISBN: 0-9708604-0-4

Edited, Designed, and Manufactured by
Favorite Recipes® Press
an imprint of

FRP

P.O. Box 305142, Nashville, Tennessee 37230
1-800-358-0560

Managing Editor: Mary Cummings
Art Director: Steve Newman
Designers: Brad Whitfield, Susan Breining
Book Project Manager: Linda A. Jones
Production Director: Mark Sloan

First Printing: 2001   5,000 copies
Second Printing: 2003   5,000 copies
Third Printing: 2006   6,000 copies

Printed in China

Introduction

Junior League cookbooks are a living legacy of tried-and-true recipes passed down generation to generation, friend to friend. True to this tradition, our recipes are a reflection of who we are, our community, and how we enjoy our lives here. This book gives our members an opportunity to sit down with you in your kitchen and share some of our favorite recipes. Some are old favorites; others are new favorites using ingredients popular today. Some you will use on a regular basis; others you may use only on those special occasions. Simple or elaborate, there is something in our cookbook for every chef. So turn a page or two and stay for a culinary visit with new friends. Our League's focus has always included women and children and has been expanded to strengthening the family. Using food is a sneaky, yet delicious way of accomplishing this goal. Nothing can bind people together more quickly than the shared experience of a good meal. **AT YOUR SERVICE** has been a labor of love for us—a love of food, family, and our community. Hopefully, we will inspire a fun family meal, a romantic picnic, or a night spent with good wine and good friends.

Start new traditions. Renew a past cooking skill you thought you'd lost.

With your purchase, you are contributing to the betterment of our community.

We thank you and are forever At Your Service.

COOKBOOK COMMITTEE

Sue Alston	Jennifer Horton
Jill Bernhardt	Jan Hughes
Molly Burke	Nancy Van Patten
Cindy Ehmer	Sandy Willyerd
Peggy Woods—Sustainer Rep	

COOKBOOK REPRINT COMMITTEES

Jo Dills	Patricia Tyson
Kristin Evans	Margaret Ward
Becky Carson	Shantel Cowan
Jennifer Horton—Sustainer Rep	

Our Mission Statement

The Junior League of Gwinnett and North Fulton Counties is a non-profit organization of women dedicated to voluntarism. We are committed to developing the potential of women through training, leadership opportunities, and service. Our purpose is to strengthen our community by creating and implementing collaborative volunteer projects.

Our Vision Statement

As an advocate of families, the Junior League of Gwinnett and North Fulton Counties will strengthen our community by embracing diverse populations, building partnerships, and inspiring shared solutions.

Membership Policy

The Junior League of Gwinnett and North Fulton Counties reaches out to women of all races, religions, and national origins who demonstrate an interest in and commitment to voluntarism.

Cookbook Mission Statement

Our objective is to create a useful, award-worthy community cookbook. AT YOUR SERVICE will reflect our members' desire to serve our community and showcase their flair for food and entertaining. Proceeds from the sale of this cookbook will provide funding for our Junior League of Gwinnett and North Fulton Counties' projects.

Acknowledgements

ABOUT OUR COVER ARTIST

Elaine Jackson is a native Georgian who lives in Alpharetta with her husband
and two children. After studying commercial art in school and working in the
advertising field, Elaine moved on to work as a watercolor artist specializing
in subjects ranging from fruits and florals to architecture, landscapes, and gardens.
She is well known in Europe through her work with a publisher for a division
of Hallmark cards. Her originals and limited edition prints are found in
public and private collections worldwide.
She specializes in commissioned work on homes and still life watercolors.
Elaine is a member of the National Watercolor Society and, locally,
the Roswell Fine Arts Association.

A SPECIAL THANK YOU TO

Collins and Arnold Construction Company for the use of their office facilities
during the preparation and distribution of this book.

Table of Contents

Throughout AT YOUR SERVICE, look for these symbols:

Our signals an important cooking tip or fun fact about the recipes in that chapter.

Our denotes a great idea for entertaining or menu suggestions that pertain to that chapter.

Our showcases wine suggestions for specific recipes.

Our own logo highlights information about our Junior League and its history, fund-raisers, and community service.

Northeastern Fulton County

The colorfully named former farming communities of Shakerag, Warsaw, and Ocee now boast a bumper crop of children, not cotton. Burgeoning commerce has led to these bedroom communities becoming one of the fastest growing areas in Atlanta. The majority of our League's membership resides here. The diverse population gives back to the community with strong participation in their local schools and places of worship.

Community landmarks include the Warsaw-Ocee Arts Center, Autry Mill Nature Preserve, and Ocee and Webb Bridge Parks. Upscale shopping centers indulge residents in the sport of bargain hunting. Children's activities, tennis, and golf are top recreational choices for families.

The PGA Tour and the ATP Tour have brought world-class professional golf and tennis athletes to the area. Competitions have been played out on the greens and the courts of local country clubs. Fans pack the grandstands to cheer on the likes of Tiger Woods, Pete Sampras, and Andre Agassi.

Elaine Jackson

Appetizers

Sun-Dried Tomato Brie

1 round Brie cheese
1 cup Pesto Sauce (below)
1 (3-ounce) jar oil-pack sun-dried tomatoes, chopped
1/2 cup fresh basil, chopped
1/2 cup pine nuts

Cut the cheese horizontally into 4 thin circles. Arrange on a serving plate.
Spread each circle with Pesto Sauce. Sprinkle with sun-dried tomatoes and
basil. Top with the pine nuts. Serve with crackers.

Makes 4 rounds

Pesto Sauce

2 cups fresh basil leaves, chopped
1/2 cup olive oil
2 garlic cloves, chopped
1 cup grated Parmesan cheese
1/2 cup pine nuts or pecans

Process the basil, olive oil, garlic, Parmesan cheese and pine nuts in a blender or
food processor until smooth.

Makes 1 cup

Raspberry Pecan Baked Brie

1 (8-ounce) round Brie cheese
1/4 cup red raspberry preserves
1/4 cup chopped pecans
1 frozen puff pastry sheet, thawed
1 egg, beaten
Garnish: 1 cup fresh red raspberries (1/2 pint)

Cut the cheese into halves horizontally. Spread the raspberry preserves on one-half of the cheese. Sprinkle with the pecans. Top with the remaining half of the cheese. Place in the center of the pastry sheet and wrap to enclose. Place on a baking sheet. Brush with the beaten egg. Bake at 400 degrees for 5 to 7 minutes or until golden brown. Garnish with the raspberries. Serve with a sliced baguette, crackers or gingersnaps.

Serves 4 to 6

Swiss Bacon Cheese Dip

1 cup shredded Swiss cheese
8 ounces cream cheese, softened
1/2 cup mayonnaise
8 slices bacon, cooked, crumbled
1/2 cup butter cracker crumbs

Combine the Swiss cheese, cream cheese and mayonnaise in a bowl and mix well. Spread in a buttered 8x8-inch baking dish. Layer the bacon and cracker crumbs over the cheese mixture. Bake at 350 degrees for 20 minutes. Serve with assorted crackers.

Serves 8 to 10

Hot Artichoke Dip

1 (14-ounce) can artichoke hearts, drained, chopped
8 ounces cream cheese, softened
1/4 teaspoon Worcestershire sauce
1 cup grated Parmesan cheese
1 cup mayonnaise
1/2 teaspoon garlic powder

Combine the artichoke hearts, cream cheese, Worcestershire sauce, Parmesan cheese, mayonnaise and garlic powder in a bowl and mix well. Spoon into a greased baking dish. Bake at 350 degrees for 25 to 30 minutes or until bubbly. Serve with melba toast.

Serves 8 to 10

Note: To make your own Melba Toast, place 1 very thin loaf of white bread on a baking sheet. Spray with nonstick cooking spray and sprinkle with garlic salt. Bake at 250 degrees until light brown. Cut into squares or desired shapes.

Cheese Ring

1 pound sharp Cheddar cheese, grated
1 cup pecans, chopped
3/4 cup mayonnaise
1 medium onion, grated
1 garlic clove, pressed
1/2 teaspoon Tabasco sauce
1 cup strawberry preserves or green pepper jelly

Combine the Cheddar cheese, pecans, mayonnaise, onion, garlic and Tabasco sauce in a bowl and mix well. Shape into a ring on a serving platter. Chill, covered, until ready to serve. Fill the center with the preserves. Serve with assorted crackers.

Serves 10 to 12

French Quarter Cheese Spread

8 ounces cream cheese, softened
1 tablespoon grated onion
1 garlic clove, minced
1/4 cup packed dark brown sugar
1/4 cup (1/2 stick) butter
1 teaspoon Worcestershire sauce
1/2 teaspoon prepared mustard
1 cup pecans, finely chopped

Combine the cream cheese, onion and garlic in a bowl and mix well using a fork. Shape into a 6-inch mound on a serving platter. Chill, covered, in the refrigerator.

Combine the brown sugar, butter, Worcestershire sauce, mustard and pecans in a saucepan. Cook over medium heat until the butter and sugar melt, stirring frequently. Uncover the cheese mound and pour the pecan mixture over the top. Chill, covered, until ready to serve. Serve at room temperature with your favorite crackers.

Serves 12

Bleu Cheese Dip

8 ounces bleu cheese, crumbled
2 garlic cloves, chopped
1/3 cup olive oil
1 tablespoon lemon juice
1/2 cup chopped red onion
1/2 cup minced parsley
Pepper to taste

Combine the bleu cheese, garlic, olive oil, lemon juice, onion, parsley and pepper in a bowl and mix well. Chill, covered, until ready to serve. Serve with crackers and apple slices.

Serves 8 to 10

Chili Cheese Dip

1 pound ground beef
1 pound Velveeta cheese
1 pound Mexican Velveeta cheese
1 (15-ounce) can chili without beans
1 (16-ounce) jar salsa

Brown the ground beef in a skillet, stirring until crumbly; drain. Place the Velveeta cheese and Mexican Velveeta cheese in a microwave-safe bowl. Microwave on High until melted. Add the ground beef, chili and salsa and mix well. Serve with your favorite chips for dipping.

Serves 20

Note: Place in a slow cooker to keep warm while serving.

Fiesta Dip

3 medium ripe avocados
3 tablespoons lemon juice
1 envelope taco seasoning mix
1 cup sour cream
1/2 cup mayonnaise
1 (15-ounce) can jalapeño refried beans
6 green onions, chopped
3 tomatoes, seeded, chopped
1 (7-ounce) can black olives, drained, chopped
8 ounces Cheddar cheese, shredded

Cut the avocados into halves and remove the seeds. Scoop the pulp into a bowl and mash. Stir in the lemon juice and 1/2 of the taco seasoning mix. Combine the sour cream, mayonnaise and remaining taco seasoning mix in a bowl and mix well.

To assemble, spread the refried beans in an 8×11-inch glass dish. Layer the avocado mixture, sour cream mixture, green onions, tomatoes and black olives over the refried beans. Sprinkle with the Cheddar cheese. Serve with tortilla chips.

Serves 12

Feel Like a Fiesta?

Cinco de Mayo—Spanish for May 5—is the Mexican national holiday that recognizes the day Mexican troops defeated Napoleon's forces. It has also become a great excuse for serving up delicious Tex-Mex food and fun for your guests.

Host an informal gathering featuring spicy appetizers like the ones on these pages, and quench everyone's thirst with the Grand Margarita (page 29) at the end of this chapter.

A piñata is a kitschy way to break the ice—fill it with candy or party favors and let each person take a swing at cracking it open.

Cinco de Mayo is a great excuse for serving up delicious Tex-Mex food.

Mexican Caviar

2 (15-ounce) cans black beans, rinsed, drained
2 (11-ounce) cans Mexicorn
3 tomatoes, seeded, chopped
4 avocados, seeded, chopped
2 red onions, chopped
6 scallions, chopped
1/2 cup vegetable oil or olive oil
1/4 cup white vinegar
2 envelopes Italian salad dressing mix

Combine the black beans, Mexicorn, tomatoes, avocados, red onions and scallions in a large bowl and mix well. Mix the vegetable oil, vinegar and salad dressing mix in a small bowl. Pour over the black bean mixture and toss to coat. Serve with tortilla chips.

Serves 20 to 24

Note: This recipe can be stored in the refrigerator for up to 5 days. It can easily be halved for a smaller gathering.

Black-Eyed Pea Dip

1 (15-ounce) can black-eyed peas, drained
1 tablespoon chopped jalapeño chiles
1/4 cup chopped onion
1/4 cup sour cream
2 tablespoons picante sauce
1 cup shredded Cheddar cheese

Mash the peas slightly with a fork in a medium bowl, leaving some chunks. Add the jalapeño chiles, onion, sour cream, picante sauce and Cheddar cheese and mix well. Spoon into an 8- or 9-inch square glass baking dish. Bake at 350 degrees for 20 to 30 minutes or until bubbly. Serve with tortilla chips.

Serves 6 to 8

Note: Do not use a blender to mash the peas in this recipe.

Baked Vidalia Onion Dip

3 cups finely chopped Vidalia onions
3 cups Swiss cheese, shredded
2^1/$_2$ cups mayonnaise
Garlic salt to taste

Combine the onions, Swiss cheese, mayonnaise and garlic salt in a bowl and mix well. Spoon into a 2^1/$_2$-quart baking dish. Bake, uncovered, at 350 degrees for 35 to 40 minutes or until bubbly. Serve warm with your favorite crackers.

Serves 6 to 8

Vidalia Onion Spread

2 cups water
^{1}/$_2$ cup vinegar
1 cup sugar
5 or 6 Vidalia onions, chopped, grated or sliced
^{1}/$_2$ cup mayonnaise
1 teaspoon celery seeds

Mix the water, vinegar and sugar in a small bowl. Pour over the onions in an airtight medium container. Marinate, covered, in the refrigerator for 4 hours or longer; drain. Add the mayonnaise and celery seeds and toss to mix well. Serve with your favorite crackers.

Serves 6 to 8

Bread Bowl Basics

The classic round loaf of bread makes a delicious presentation for dip-style appetizers. To make, slice off the top quarter of the bread loaf with a serrated bread knife. Hollow out the bottom section, leaving a 1-inch shell. Cut the bread top and inside pieces into approximately 1-inch cubes. Place the bread shell and bread cubes on a baking sheet. Bake at 350 degrees for 12 minutes or until light brown. Baking the shell and bread cubes will add a toasted flavor. Let cool, then spoon prepared dip into the bread bowl. Use the bread cubes for dipping. Sourdough, pumpernickel, and Italian peasant bread are also delicious.

Baking the shell and bread cubes will add a toasted flavor.

Green Salsa

1 tomato, chopped
4 green onions, chopped
1 (4-ounce) can chopped green chiles, drained
1 (4-ounce) can sliced black olives, drained
1 cup shredded Monterey Jack cheese
$1/2$ cup Italian salad dressing

Combine the tomato, green onions, green chiles, black olives and cheese in a bowl and mix well. Add the salad dressing and toss to coat. Chill, covered, until ready to serve.

Serves 6 to 8

Fresh Salsa

8 medium tomatoes, chopped, or 4 beefsteak tomatoes, chopped
1 (16-ounce) can tomato sauce
1 (10-ounce) can diced tomatoes with green chiles
1 large purple onion, finely chopped
Juice of 1 lime
4 to 8 jalapeño chiles, finely chopped, or to taste
2 or 3 garlic cloves, pressed
1 bunch fresh cilantro, trimmed, snipped
2 tablespoons snipped fresh oregano leaves, or 2 teaspoons dried oregano
$1/2$ to 1 teaspoon cumin
Salt and pepper to taste

Combine the tomatoes, tomato sauce, tomatoes with green chiles, onion and lime juice in a large bowl and mix well. Add the jalapeño chiles, garlic, cilantro, oregano, cumin, salt and pepper and mix well. Serve with tortilla chips.

Serves 6 to 8

Fruit Salsa with Cinnamon Sugar Chips

1 or 2 apples, cored, chopped
1 pint strawberries, chopped
3 kiwifruit, chopped, or other seasonal fruit
1 tablespoon (heaping) apple jelly
1 tablespoon orange juice
1/2 teaspoon grated orange zest
Cinnamon Sugar Chips (below)

Mix the apples, strawberries and kiwifruit in a bowl. Stir in the jelly, orange juice and orange zest gently. Chill, covered, until ready to serve. Serve with Cinnamon Sugar Chips.

Serves 6 to 8

Cinnamon Sugar Chips

10 flour tortillas
Cinnamon sugar to taste

Brush each tortilla lightly with water. Sprinkle with cinnamon sugar. Cut into chip-size pieces. Place on a baking sheet sprayed lightly with nonstick cooking spray. Bake at 350 degrees for 10 minutes or until crisp.

Serves 6 to 8

Note: Cinnamon sugar can be purchased in the spice section of the grocery store or made by adding 3 to 4 tablespoons cinnamon per 1/2 cup sugar.

The Junior League's Signature Style

One of the strengths of the Junior League is its ability to identify a need in the community and implement a program to assist that need. These become known as our "signature" projects. Our first signature project was Project Self-Esteem, an in-school program implemented to boost self-image in elementary and middle school children. Project Self-Esteem began in 1988 at Berkeley Lake Elementary School and expanded to sixteen schools in Gwinnett and North Fulton. Our latest signature project was the "W.I.S.E." Center, an education, training, and family life skills project for women who have overcome domestic violence and are making a new start for themselves and their children.

Amaretto Fruit Dip

8 ounces cream cheese, softened
1 (7-ounce) jar marshmallow creme
2 tablespoons amaretto

Combine the cream cheese, marshmallow creme and amaretto in a mixing bowl and beat until creamy. Serve with favorite fruits that have been dipped in lemon juice to preserve color.

Makes about 2 cups

Crab Meat Spread

8 ounces cream cheese, softened
2 tablespoons crumbled bleu cheese
1 tablespoon lemon juice
$1^1/_4$ tablespoons chopped onion
$^1/_8$ teaspoon garlic powder
5 ounces chili sauce or cocktail sauce
3 tablespoons prepared horseradish
1 (7-ounce) can crab meat

Mix the cream cheese, bleu cheese, lemon juice, onion and garlic powder in a bowl. Spread the cheese mixture on a platter. Mix the chili sauce and horseradish in a small bowl and pour over the cheese mixture. Spread the crab meat over the top. Serve with unsalted crackers.

Serves 6 to 8

Note: For extra flavor and festive color, add finely chopped herbs such as parsley or basil to the sauce. Chopped scallions sprinkled over the spread and around the platter also make a pretty presentation.

Hot Crab Dip

8 ounces cream cheese, softened
3 tablespoons mayonnaise
2 tablespoons lemon juice
1 teaspoon Worcestershire sauce
1 tablespoon prepared horseradish
$^1/_2$ teaspoon Old Bay seasoning
2 scallions, chopped
8 ounces lump crab meat, drained

Melt the cream cheese in a saucepan over low heat, stirring constantly until smooth. Stir in the mayonnaise, lemon juice, Worcestershire sauce, horseradish and Old Bay seasoning. Add the scallions and crab meat. Cook until heated through. Serve warm with your favorite crackers.

Makes 2$^1/_2$ cups

Smoked Oyster Dip

8 ounces cream cheese, softened
1$^1/_2$ cups mayonnaise
Tabasco sauce or hot sauce to taste
1 tablespoon lemon juice
1 (4-ounce) can chopped black olives, drained
1 (3-ounce) can smoked oysters, drained, chopped

Combine the cream cheese, mayonnaise, Tabasco sauce and lemon juice in a medium bowl. Stir in the olives and oysters. Spoon into a serving bowl. Serve with fresh vegetables, pita chips or crackers.

Makes 3 cups

Beat the Big Chill with Island Heat

Got cabin fever? Get island-happy and have a luau in winter. Raise folded tables on bricks high enough for everyone to slide their knees under, then seat guests on cushions on the floor, Hawaiian-style. Decorate with leis, flowers, and pineapples. Have people wear their favorite tacky tourist attire.

Start with seafood-based appetizers like the ones here. For the main course, serve Smoked Sesame Tenderloin (page 88) or Island Barbecued Spareribs (page 91) from our Entrées chapter. Don't forget the umbrella drinks!

Get island-happy and have a luau in winter.

Shrimp and Bleu Cheese

2$\frac{1}{2}$ pounds unpeeled shrimp, boiled, peeled
4 ounces bleu cheese, crumbled
1 onion, thinly sliced
$\frac{1}{4}$ cup olive oil
Cajun seasoning to taste

Combine the shrimp, bleu cheese and onion in a bowl and toss to mix well.
Add the olive oil and Cajun seasoning and mix well. Marinate, covered, in the
refrigerator for 24 hours. Serve with crackers.

Serves 6 to 8

Pesto Pinwheels

12 ounces cream cheese, softened
1 cup grated Parmesan cheese
3 green onions, chopped
$\frac{1}{2}$ cup basil pesto
1 cup chopped black olives
1 (16-ounce) package frozen puff pastry, slightly thawed

Combine the cream cheese, Parmesan cheese, green onions, pesto and olives in a
bowl and mix well. Roll each puff pastry sheet into a 10×16-inch rectangle on a
lightly floured surface. Spread the cream cheese mixture evenly over each sheet
and roll up, beginning at the long side. Wrap in freezer paper. Freeze for 3 hours
or up to 3 months. Remove from the freezer and thaw for 30 minutes. Unwrap
and cut into $\frac{1}{4}$-inch rounds. Place on lightly greased baking sheets. Bake at
350 degrees for 10 to 12 minutes or until golden brown. Serve warm.

Makes about 100

Note: There are 2 sheets of puff pastry in each package.

Mexican Roll-Ups

8 ounces cream cheese, softened
1 cup sour cream
1 (4-ounce) can diced black olives, drained
2 cups grated Cheddar cheese
1 (10-ounce) can diced tomatoes with green chiles, drained
10 (8-inch) flour tortillas
Peach salsa, your favorite salsa or picante sauce for dipping

Mix the cream cheese and sour cream with a fork in a bowl until smooth.
Stir in the black olives, Cheddar cheese and tomatoes with green chiles.
Spread thinly over the tortillas. Roll up tightly and place in an airtight
container. Chill, covered, for 4 to 12 hours. Cut into 1-inch rounds using
a sharp knife. Arrange on a serving platter around a bowl of peach salsa
for dipping.

Makes 80

BLT Bites

24 cherry tomatoes
1 pound bacon, crisp-cooked, crumbled
1/2 cup chopped green onions
1/2 cup mayonnaise

Cut off the top of each tomato opposite the stem end. Scoop out the
inside to form a shell. Drain upside down on paper towels. Combine the
bacon, green onions and mayonnaise in a bowl. Spoon inside the tomato
shells. Chill until ready to serve.

Makes 24

Tipsy Dogs

1 cup bourbon
1 cup ketchup
1¹/₂ cups packed brown sugar
3 pounds cocktail franks

Mix the bourbon, ketchup and brown sugar in a large roasting pan. Add the cocktail franks. Bake, covered, at 300 degrees for 3 hours, stirring every 30 minutes.

Serves 15 to 20

Note: May be prepared ahead and reheated before serving.

Cheese Straws

15 ounces extra-sharp Cheddar cheese, grated
³/₄ cup (1¹/₂ sticks) butter or margarine
2 cups flour
1¹/₄ teaspoons baking powder
¹/₂ teaspoon salt
5 to 6 dashes of Tabasco sauce
1 teaspoon cayenne pepper

Let the cheese and butter stand at room temperature until softened. Sift the flour, baking powder and salt together. Mix the cheese and butter in a bowl with your hands. Add the Tabasco sauce, cayenne pepper and flour mixture and mix well. Place in a cookie press fitted with the star tip. Press into 2-inch lengths on ungreased baking sheets. Bake at 300 degrees for 15 minutes. Reduce the oven temperature to 225 degrees. Bake for 10 to 30 minutes longer or until crisp.

Makes about 120

Note: Bake the cheese straws slowly to achieve crispness. If the cheese straws are baking too fast, leave the oven door open. You may also freeze after baking. For special occasions, roll the dough ¹/₈ inch thick on a lightly floured surface. Cut into desired shapes with cookie cutters.

Jalapeño Cheese Bites

4 cups shredded Cheddar cheese
4 eggs, beaten
1 (2-ounce) jar chopped pimentos, drained
3 canned jalapeño chiles, seeded, chopped
1 teaspoon minced onion

Combine the cheese, eggs, pimentos, jalapeño chiles and onion in a medium bowl and mix well. Spread in a lightly greased 8×8-inch baking dish. Bake at 350 degrees for 30 to 40 minutes or until set. Remove from the oven and let stand for 10 minutes. Cut into bite-size squares. Serve immediately.

Makes 3 dozen

Sausage-Stuffed Mushrooms

1 pound large white mushrooms
1 pound ground spicy sausage
8 ounces cream cheese, softened

Rinse the mushrooms and remove the stems; pat dry. Brown the sausage in a skillet over medium heat, stirring until crumbly; drain. Stir in the cream cheese. Spoon into the mushroom caps using a teaspoon or melon baller. Place in a 9×13-inch baking pan sprayed with nonstick cooking spray. Cover with foil. Bake at 350 degrees for 30 to 40 minutes or until heated through.

Makes 30 to 60 depending on the size of the mushrooms

Spiced Iced Tea

3 quarts unsweetened brewed tea
12 ounces frozen lemonade concentrate, thawed
1$\frac{1}{2}$ cups sugar
1 quart ginger ale
Garnish:
Lemon slices

Combine the tea, lemonade concentrate and sugar in a large pitcher and stir until the sugar is dissolved. Chill until ready to serve. Add the ginger ale just before serving. Pour over ice in glasses. Garnish with lemon slices.

Makes 1 gallon

Bourbon Slush

2 family-size tea bags
1 cup boiling water
$\frac{3}{4}$ cup sugar
3 cups water
1 (6-ounce) can lemonade concentrate, thawed
1 (6-ounce) can orange juice concentrate, thawed
$\frac{1}{2}$ to 1 cup bourbon
Ginger ale

Steep the tea bags in 1 cup boiling water in a 4-cup liquid measure for 5 minutes. Remove and discard the tea bags. Combine the tea, sugar, 3 cups water, lemonade concentrate, orange juice concentrate and bourbon in a large freezer container and mix well. Freeze, covered, for 8 to 12 hours. To serve, spoon the mixture into glasses and add enough ginger ale to fill.

Serves 16

Delightful Punch

4 cups sugar
6 cups water
2 cups pineapple juice
1 cup lemon juice
4 cups orange juice
2 quarts ginger ale

Bring the sugar and water to a boil in a saucepan. Boil for 2 minutes. Remove from the heat and let stand until cool. Mix with the pineapple juice, lemon juice and orange juice in a large freezer container. Freeze, covered, for 10 to 12 hours. Remove from the freezer 1 hour before serving. Place in a punch bowl. Add the ginger ale just before serving.

Makes 5 to 6 quarts

Southern Comfort Punch

6 lemons, thinly sliced
4 navel oranges, thinly sliced
2 (6-ounce) cans frozen lemonade concentrate
1 (6-ounce) can frozen orange juice concentrate
2 liters Sprite
1 liter Southern Comfort

Place the lemon and orange slices in single layers on baking sheets. Freeze for 2 to 2¹/₂ hours. Combine the lemonade concentrate, orange juice concentrate, Sprite and Southern Comfort in a punch bowl just before serving. Add several cups of ice. Float the frozen fruit slices on top.

Makes 3 liters

Gin Fizz

1 cup frozen lemonade concentrate
1 cup 2% milk
1 cup gin

Combine the lemonade concentrate, milk and gin in a blender container. Add some ice and process until frothy. Pour into serving glasses. Serve with brunch or as a cool summer cocktail in Champagne flutes.

Serves 2

Note: Make the quantity you desire by using equal portions of all the ingredients.

Island Mimosa

1 (12-ounce) can apricot nectar
1 (12-ounce) can pineapple juice
1 (6-ounce) can frozen orange juice concentrate, thawed
3/4 cup water
1 (750-milliliter) bottle Champagne, chilled
Garnish: Fresh strawberries

Combine the apricot nectar, pineapple juice, orange juice concentrate and water in a large pitcher and stir to mix well. Chill, covered, in the refrigerator. Stir in the Champagne gently before serving. Pour into serving glasses and garnish with fresh strawberries.

Makes 2 quarts

Grand Margarita

3 ounces Sweet-and-Sour Mix (below)
1¼ ounces tequila
1 ounce Triple Sec
Dash of orange juice
1 lime wedge
Kosher salt or other coarse salt
⅓ teaspoon Grand Marnier
Garnish: Lime wedge

Combine the Sweet-and-Sour Mix, tequila, Triple Sec and orange juice in a shaker and shake to mix well. To serve, rub the rim of a glass with a lime wedge. Invert and swirl in kosher salt in a small bowl. Pour the cocktail into the prepared glass. Top with a float of Grand Marnier. Garnish with a lime wedge. Ole!

Serves 1

Sweet-and-Sour Mix

2 cups freshly squeezed lemon juice (about 10 lemons)
2 cups freshly squeezed lime juice (about 12 limes)
3 cups sugar
3 cups water

Combine the lemon juice, lime juice, sugar and water in a 4-quart saucepan. Heat over medium-high heat until the sugar dissolves. Remove from the heat and cool. Store in the refrigerator.

Makes 2 quarts, or enough for about 16 servings

A Margarita and Tequila Primer

Whether you like 'em frozen or on the rocks, salted or plain, the margarita is a party in a glass.

When you're planning the next neighborhood fiesta, serve a sampling of premium tequilas to complement all those frosty margaritas. To help you sort out the varieties, choose one from each category here:

* Blanco—fresh, unaged tequila to be enjoyed with a twist of lime or in a margarita
* Reposado—aged in oak barrels at least two months; smooth and flavorful
* Añejo—aged at least one year in oak barrels; can be compared to the darkness and complexity of fine whiskey or Cognac—sip and savor in a snifter, not in a mixed drink.

When you're planning the next neighborhood fiesta, serve a sampling of premium tequilas to complement all those frosty margaritas.

Duluth and Suwanee

Both of these small towns feature a historic town square and strong ties to the railroad that runs through them. Newcomers and natives alike are flocking to the shops that are blossoming throughout these communities in western Gwinnett County. The population is booming, too, as corporations relocate employees and their families from all over the world to this popular area. Duluth and Suwanee residents give back to their communities by being heavily involved in their schools and organizations that help others less fortunate. One such organization is the Duluth Cooperative Ministry, a coalition of churches that operates a food bank and lends additional assistance to families in need. Suwanee has been identified by the Georgia Department of Community Affairs as a "Better Hometown," and Suwanee citizens can now receive help in revitalizing their Old Town historic district.

This is a region that plays as hard as it works. Many residents enjoy boating and floating on nearby Lake Lanier and the Chattahoochee River. The Gwinnett Civic Center is a hot spot for meetings, shows, concerts, and the arts. Interstate highway I-85 has become a power shopping corridor, with Gwinnett Place, the Mall of Georgia, and other shopping centers lining it as it runs through the county.

Breads and Breakfast

Sour Cream Corn Bread

1 tablespoon vegetable oil
1 cup sour cream
1 cup cream-style corn
1/4 cup vegetable oil
1 cup cornmeal
2 eggs
1/2 cup shredded cheese (optional)
1/4 cup finely chopped jalapeño chiles (optional)

Pour 1 tablespoon vegetable oil into an 8-inch cast-iron skillet, using a paper towel to evenly distribute the oil. Place in a 400-degree oven. Combine the sour cream, corn, 1/4 cup vegetable oil, cornmeal and eggs in a medium mixing bowl and mix well. Stir in the cheese and jalapeño chiles. Remove the preheated skillet from the oven. Add the batter. Bake for 30 to 35 minutes or until golden brown.

Serves 8

Note: If you don't have a cast-iron skillet, spoon the batter into muffin cups and bake for 20 minutes.

Pan of Biscuits

2 cups self-rising flour
1/8 teaspoon baking soda
1/2 teaspoon salt
3 tablespoons shortening

1 to 1 2/3 cups milk or buttermilk
1/4 cup all-purpose flour
1 tablespoon butter, melted

Mix the self-rising flour, baking soda and salt in a bowl. Cut in the shortening until crumbly. Add enough milk to form a moist dough that resembles cottage cheese. Spoon the dough in biscuit-size portions onto the all-purpose flour on a plate. Cover each portion with the all-purpose flour and shake off the excess. Place each portion close together in a 9-inch round baking pan sprayed with nonstick cooking spray. Brush the tops with the butter. Bake at 475 degrees for 15 to 20 minutes or until golden brown.

Makes 1 dozen biscuits

Quick Biscuits

1 cup baking mix
1/2 cup sour cream
1/4 cup (1/2 stick) butter, melted

Combine the baking mix, sour cream and butter in a bowl and mix well. Spoon into greased muffin cups. Bake at 350 degrees for 20 to 25 minutes or until golden brown.

Makes 6 large biscuits

Note: Perfect to serve with casual soup-and-salad meals.

Angel Biscuits

1 envelope active dry yeast
1/4 cup warm water
5 cups flour
1/4 cup sugar
1 tablespoon baking powder
2 teaspoons salt
1 teaspoon baking soda
1 cup shortening
2 cups buttermilk

Dissolve the yeast in the warm water in a 1-cup liquid measure. Mix the flour, sugar, baking powder, salt and baking soda in a large bowl. Cut in the shortening until crumbly. Add the yeast mixture and buttermilk and stir to form a soft dough. Roll lightly 1/2 inch thick on a lightly floured surface. Cut with a biscuit cutter, dipping the cutter in flour between cuts. Place 1 inch apart on a baking sheet sprayed with nonstick cooking spray. Bake at 400 degrees for 12 to 14 minutes or until golden brown. Brush with melted butter if desired. Serve warm.

Makes 1 1/2 dozen biscuits

Volunteer "Angels" for a Day

On August 20, 1994, seven of our members drove to Albany, Georgia, and spent the day helping an 88-year-old flood victim who had been displaced from her home. The volunteers carried rotting wallboard, framework, and other debris out of the house, which they tried to make livable again. This hard day's work became the League's first official Done In A Day (DIAD) project.

League members volunteering on this committee spend one or two weekend days or evenings each month completing short-term community service projects. Our DIAD projects have included Christmas in April, Gwinnett County Senior Services, Habitat for Humanity, Gwinnett Children's Shelter, North Fulton and Gwinnett DFACS, and Annandale Village.

Apple Bread

3 cups flour
1 teaspoon baking soda
1 teaspoon salt
1 teaspoon cinnamon
$1/4$ teaspoon baking powder
3 cups shredded peeled Golden Delicious, Rome Beauty or Jonathan apples
    (4 medium apples)
3 eggs, beaten
2 cups sugar
$2/3$ cup vegetable oil
1 teaspoon vanilla extract

Grease and flour 3 medium or 2 large loaf pans. Mix the flour, baking soda, salt, cinnamon and baking powder in a bowl. Combine the apples, eggs, sugar, oil and vanilla in a large mixing bowl and mix well. Add the flour mixture and stir until moistened. Pour into the prepared pans. Bake at 325 degrees for 45 to 55 minutes or until a wooden pick inserted in the center comes out clean. Cool in the pans for 10 minutes. Invert onto wire racks to cool completely. Wrap in foil. Store for 8 to 12 hours before slicing.

Makes 2 or 3 loaves

Grandma Ree's Banana Nut Bread

2½ cups flour
½ cup sugar
½ cup packed brown sugar
3½ teaspoons baking powder
1 teaspoon salt

3 tablespoons vegetable oil
⅓ cup milk
1 egg
3 medium bananas, mashed
1 cup walnuts, chopped

Grease the bottom of a 5×9-inch pan. Combine the flour, sugar, brown sugar, baking powder, salt, oil, milk, egg and bananas in a mixing bowl. Beat for 30 seconds. Stir in the walnuts. Pour into the prepared pan. Bake at 350 degrees for 65 to 70 minutes or until the loaf tests done. Cool in the pan. Loosen from the sides of the pan and remove to a wire rack.

Makes 1 loaf

Banana Chocolate Nut Bread

4 cups flour
2 teaspoons baking soda
¼ teaspoon salt
1 cup (2 sticks) butter or
    margarine, softened

2 cups sugar
4 eggs
6 ripe bananas, mashed
1 cup finely chopped nuts
1 cup (6 ounces) chocolate chips

Sift the flour, baking soda and salt together. Cream the butter and sugar in a mixing bowl until light and fluffy. Add the eggs 1 at a time, beating well after each addition. Beat in the flour mixture. Stir in the bananas, nuts and chocolate chips. Pour into 2 greased and floured 5×9-inch loaf pans. Bake at 300 degrees for 1 hour.

Makes 2 loaves

Note: For moister bread, bake at 250 degrees for 2 hours.

Brownie Bread

1 (19-ounce) package brownie mix
1 (5.5-ounce) package buttermilk
   baking mix (1 cup)
2/3 cup water
2 eggs

1/4 cup vegetable oil
1 teaspoon vanilla extract
1 cup (6 ounces) chocolate chips
1/2 cup pecans or walnuts, chopped

Combine the brownie mix, baking mix, water, eggs, oil and vanilla in a mixing bowl and beat until blended. Stir in the chocolate chips and pecans. Pour into a 5×9-inch loaf pan sprayed with nonstick cooking spray. Bake at 350 degrees for 30 to 35 minutes or until the loaf begins to pull from the sides of the pan. Do not overbake.

Makes 1 loaf

Note: This recipe works wonderfully in miniature loaf pans. Just bake for 20 minutes, being careful not to overbake.

Pumpkin Bread

4 eggs
1 cup corn oil
2/3 cup water
2 cups cooked pumpkin
3 cups sugar
3 1/3 cups flour

2 teaspoons baking soda
1 1/2 teaspoons salt
1 teaspoon nutmeg
1 teaspoon cinnamon
1/2 cup chopped pecans (optional)

Beat the eggs well in a large mixing bowl. Add the corn oil, water and pumpkin and mix well. Add the sugar, flour, baking soda, salt, nutmeg and cinnamon, beating after each addition until blended. Stir in the pecans. Pour into 3 lightly greased small (4 1/2 × 8 1/2-inch) loaf pans. Bake at 350 degrees for 1 hour. Cool in the pans for 10 minutes. Invert onto wire racks to cool completely.

Makes 3 small loaves

Lemon Blueberry Bread

1 package bakery-style blueberry muffin mix with crumbs
2 tablespoons poppy seeds
1 egg
3/4 cup water
1 tablespoon grated lemon zest
1 tablespoon lemon juice
1/2 cup confectioners' sugar
1 tablespoon lemon juice

Drain the canned blueberries from the mix and rinse; drain. Combine the muffin mix, poppy seeds, egg, water, lemon zest and 1 tablespoon lemon juice in a mixing bowl. Beat for 50 strokes. Fold in the blueberries. Pour into a 5×9-inch loaf pan sprayed with nonstick cooking spray. Sprinkle the top with the crumbs from the mix.

Bake at 350 degrees for 1 hour or until a wooden pick inserted in the center comes out clean. Cool in the pan for 10 minutes. Loosen the loaf from the side of the pan and remove to a wire rack. Beat the confectioners' sugar and 1 tablespoon lemon juice in a bowl until smooth. Drizzle over the warm bread.

Serves 10

Small Fund-raisers Reap Big Rewards

Although the League hosts one or two major fund-raisers each year, as the membership grew, we realized we were missing other short-term opportunities. Often retail stores or community agencies would approach us to assist in grand-opening projects, art auctions, and other special events. To answer this need, we formed our Fund In A Day committee.

Some of our first events included a bake sale, Letters from Santa, and an art auction. Today, the art auction and a spring tennis tournament are two of the League's most profitable and popular events. It is as much "fun" in a day as it is "fund" in a day for our members!

Fund In A Day also helps us plan for our future by serving as an "incubator" for developing fund-raisers. If the membership decides a long-running fund-raiser is no longer viable, it will often look to the Fund In A Day committee for profitable special events that might be developed into major fund-raisers.

Orange Cranberry Bread

2$\frac{1}{2}$ cups flour
2 teaspoons baking powder
1 teaspoon baking soda
$\frac{1}{4}$ teaspoon salt
1$\frac{1}{4}$ cups sugar
$\frac{1}{2}$ cup unsweetened applesauce
3 egg whites
$\frac{1}{4}$ cup orange juice
Grated zest of 1 medium orange, or 1 teaspoon dried orange peel
1 teaspoon vanilla extract
1 cup fresh cranberries, chopped, or $\frac{1}{2}$ cup dried cranberries

Sift the flour, baking powder, baking soda and salt together. Combine the sugar, applesauce, egg whites, orange juice, orange zest, vanilla and cranberries in a large mixing bowl and beat well. Add the flour mixture and stir gently until moistened. Pour into a 5×9-inch loaf pan sprayed with nonstick cooking spray. Bake at 350 degrees for 50 minutes. Cool in the pan for 10 minutes and remove to a wire rack. Serve warm.

Serves 10

Note: Each serving has less than $\frac{1}{2}$ gram of fat.

Strawberry Bread and Butter

2 (10-ounce) packages frozen strawberries, thawed
3 cups flour
1 teaspoon baking soda
1 teaspoon salt
1 teaspoon cinnamon
2 cups sugar
3 eggs, well beaten
1¼ cups vegetable oil
1½ cups pecans, chopped
¼ cup (½ stick) butter, softened
½ cup confectioners' sugar

Drain the strawberries, reserving the juice. Mix the flour, baking soda, salt, cinnamon and sugar in a large mixing bowl. Make a well in the center. Add the eggs and oil and stir just until moistened. Stir in the strawberries and pecans. Spoon into 2 greased medium loaf pans. Bake at 350 degrees for 1 hour. Cool in the pans for 10 minutes. Remove to wire racks.

For the strawberry butter, process the butter and confectioners' sugar in a blender or food processor until creamy. Add just enough of the reserved strawberry juice to make of the desired spreading consistency. To serve, slice the warm bread and spread with the strawberry butter.

Makes 2 loaves

Layered Parmesan Loaf

1 (8-ounce) can flaky biscuits
1/4 cup (1/2 stick) butter, melted
1/4 cup grated Parmesan cheese

Separate the biscuits. Dip each in the melted butter and then in the Parmesan cheese. Arrange in 2 overlapping layers on a baking sheet. Bake at 425 degrees for 8 to 10 minutes or until golden brown.

Serves 8

Caraway Breadsticks

1/2 cup (1 stick) butter, softened
1 cup grated Parmesan cheese
1/2 cup sour cream
1 cup flour
1 tablespoon caraway seeds
1 egg white, beaten

Beat the butter in a mixing bowl until creamy. Add the Parmesan cheese and sour cream and mix well. Beat in the flour. Stir in the caraway seeds. Roll into a 7×12-inch rectangle on a lightly floured surface. Cut into strips and twist. Place on baking sheets sprayed lightly with nonstick cooking spray. Brush with the egg white. Bake at 350 degrees for 12 to 15 minutes or until golden brown.

Makes 5 dozen breadsticks

Note: This recipe is easily doubled and freezes well.

Refrigerator Bran Muffins

5 cups bran flakes (with or
  without raisins)
1¹/₂ cups sugar
2¹/₂ cups flour

2¹/₂ teaspoons baking soda
1 teaspoon salt
¹/₂ cup vegetable oil
2 cups buttermilk

Mix the bran flakes, sugar, flour, baking soda and salt in a large bowl. Stir in the oil and buttermilk. Store in an airtight container in the refrigerator for up to 6 weeks. Use as needed.

To bake, spoon the batter into 2-inch muffin cups sprayed with nonstick cooking spray. Bake at 400 degrees for 18 to 20 minutes or until golden brown.

Makes 3 dozen 2-inch muffins

Note: You may bake in miniature muffin cups and reduce the baking time by half.

Sesame Cheese Muffins

1¹/₂ cups baking mix
¹/₂ cup grated sharp Colby
  cheese
¹/₄ cup minced onion
1 tablespoon butter
1 egg, well beaten

¹/₂ cup milk
¹/₂ teaspoon garlic powder
¹/₄ cup grated sharp Colby
  cheese
1 tablespoon sesame seeds,
  toasted

Mix the baking mix and ¹/₂ cup cheese in a large bowl. Sauté the onion in the butter in a skillet until transparent. Combine with the egg, milk and garlic powder in a small bowl and mix well. Add to the cheese mixture and beat vigorously for 30 seconds. Fill 12 well-greased muffin cups ²/₃ full. Sprinkle with ¹/₄ cup cheese and sesame seeds. Bake at 400 degrees for 12 to 15 minutes or until golden brown.

Makes 1 dozen muffins

From the Wine List

Opening and taste-testing a bottle of wine isn't the exotic mystery it's cracked up to be.

To open the bottle, cut off the wrapper around the top lip and wipe the top of the cork clean. Insert the corkscrew and turn it as deeply as possible into the cork. Once you've lifted the cork one-quarter of the way out, stop and turn the corkscrew even further into the cork. Then finish pulling the cork out of the bottle. Pour the wine into a glass, swirl it, and sniff. If the wine smells like a dank cellar or moldy newspapers, it has spoiled and lost its fruity smell and taste. This is usually due to poor storage of the wine. "Corked" wine means that the cork that is supposed to seal the bottle was defective.

Opening and taste-testing a bottle of wine isn't the exotic mystery it's cracked up to be.

Breakfast Muffins

1½ cups plus 2 tablespoons flour
¾ cup sugar
2 teaspoons baking powder
¼ teaspoon salt
¼ teaspoon nutmeg
½ cup milk

1 egg, beaten
⅓ cup butter, melted
½ cup sugar
1 teaspoon cinnamon
½ teaspoon vanilla extract
⅓ cup butter, melted

Grease and flour 18 small muffin cups. Mix the flour, ¾ cup sugar, baking powder, salt and nutmeg in a bowl. Add the milk, egg and ⅓ cup butter and mix well. Fill the prepared muffin cups ½ full. Bake at 400 degrees for 20 minutes or until light brown. Mix ½ cup sugar, cinnamon and vanilla in a shallow dish. Dip each hot muffin in ⅓ cup butter and roll in the sugar mixture. Serve warm.

Makes 18 muffins

Variation: Try adding ½ cup of your favorite fruit to this recipe. It's sure to become a family favorite.

Orange Muffins

2 cups flour
1 teaspoon baking soda
1 teaspoon salt
½ cup (1 stick) butter, softened
1 cup sugar
¾ cup sour cream

1 teaspoon grated orange zest
½ cup raisins (optional)
½ cup chopped pecans
½ cup sugar
Juice of 1 orange (about ½ cup)

Sift the flour, baking soda and salt together. Cream the butter and 1 cup sugar in a mixing bowl until light and fluffy. Add the sour cream and flour mixture alternately, beating well after each addition. Fold in the orange zest, raisins and pecans. The batter will be stiff. Spoon into well-greased miniature muffin cups. Bake at 375 degrees for 12 to 15 minutes or until golden brown. Cool slightly. Mix ½ cup sugar and orange juice in a bowl. Dip each muffin in the orange juice mixture and place on wire racks to cool.

Makes 3 dozen miniature muffins

Apple Breakfast Sandwiches

1/3 cup packed brown sugar
2 tablespoons flour
1/2 teaspoon cinnamon
1 (10-ounce) can buttermilk
   biscuits

2 large apples, peeled, cored,
   sliced into 4 rings each
1 tablespoon butter, melted
1 cup shredded sharp Cheddar
   cheese

Mix the brown sugar, flour and cinnamon in a bowl. Separate the biscuits and press each into a 3-inch circle. Place on a lightly greased baking sheet. Sprinkle with the brown sugar mixture. Top with an apple ring and drizzle with butter. Sprinkle with the cheese. Bake at 350 degrees for 15 minutes. Serve immediately.

Makes 8 open-face sandwiches

Berry Cream Cheese Braid

3 ounces cream cheese
1/4 cup (1/2 stick) margarine
2 cups baking mix
1/3 cup milk

1/2 cup berry preserves
1 cup confectioners' sugar
1 to 2 tablespoons milk
1/2 teaspoon vanilla extract

Cut the cream cheese and margarine into the baking mix in a bowl with a pastry blender until crumbly. Add 1/3 cup milk and stir until moistened. Knead 8 to 10 times on a lightly floured surface. Place the dough between 2 pieces of waxed paper. Roll into a 12×18-inch rectangle. Remove the top layer of waxed paper and invert the rectangle onto a greased baking sheet; remove the waxed paper. Spread the preserves down the center of the dough. Cut 2 1/2-inch slits from the outer edge to the filling at 1 inch intervals using kitchen shears. Fold the strips alternately over the filling, sealing the ends. Bake at 425 degrees for 12 to 15 minutes or until golden brown.

For the glaze, beat the confectioners' sugar, 1 to 2 tablespoons milk and vanilla in a mixing bowl until smooth. Drizzle over the warm braid.

Serves 6

The Apples of Your Eye

At the height of apple season in late summer and fall, you'll see many local and regional varieties in the supermarket from which to choose. For cooking, tart apples such as Greenings and Granny Smiths are best—green does not necessarily mean sour. For a baked apple, you want one that will keep its shape, so try Golden Delicious, Rome Beauty, or Cortland varieties. Red Delicious and McIntosh apples are great for snacking and salads, but not for cooking. York apples are slightly tart and good for cooking and Winesaps are glossy red and make a spicy good cider. To prevent any apple variety from browning when sliced, pour 2 tablespoons of pineapple juice over the slices. It adds a nice flavor and eliminates the "yuck" factor in kids' lunches.

Cream Cheese Danish

2 (8-ounce) cans crescent rolls
1 egg yolk
1 cup sugar
16 ounces cream cheese, softened

1 teaspoon vanilla extract
1 egg white, stiffly beaten
1/4 cup sugar
1/2 cup pecans, chopped

Unroll 1 can of the crescent roll dough. Press into a lightly greased 9×13-inch baking pan. Whisk the egg yolk in a medium mixing bowl until well beaten. Add 1 cup sugar, cream cheese and vanilla and beat until smooth. Pour into the prepared pan. Unroll the remaining can of crescent roll dough and press the indentations to seal. Place over the filling. Spread the stiffly beaten egg white over the top. Sprinkle with 1/4 cup sugar and pecans. Bake at 350 degrees for 30 to 35 minutes or until golden brown.

Serves 8

Cream Cheese and Strawberry Tart

1 (1-crust) pie pastry
1 tablespoon sugar
8 ounces cream cheese, softened
1/4 cup sugar
1/2 teaspoon vanilla extract

1 egg
3 cups fresh strawberries, halved
1/4 cup white chocolate chips
1 teaspoon vegetable oil

Let the pie pastry stand at room temperature for 15 to 20 minutes. Unfold the pastry and roll into a 12-inch circle on a large baking sheet. Prick the pastry with a fork and sprinkle with 1 tablespoon sugar. Bake at 450 degrees for 8 to 10 minutes. Cool slightly. Reduce the oven temperature to 375 degrees. Beat the cream cheese, 1/4 cup sugar and vanilla in a mixing bowl until creamy. Add the egg and beat until smooth. Spread over the crust to within 1/2 inch of the edge. Bake for 13 to 18 minutes or until set in the center and light brown around the edge. Cool completely. Arrange the strawberry halves over the filling. Combine the white chocolate chips and oil in a microwave-safe bowl. Microwave on Low until melted, stirring every 30 seconds. Stir until smooth and drizzle over the strawberries. Chill, covered, until ready to serve. Cut into wedges to serve.

Serves 8

Mom's Christmas Breakfast Rolls

1/4 cup (1/2 stick) butter, melted
1/2 cup light brown sugar
1 tablespoon cinnamon
1 (24-ounce) package frozen
   dinner rolls
1 (4-ounce) package
   butterscotch cook-and-serve
   pudding mix
1/2 cup nuts, chopped
Cherries or raisins (optional)

Mix the butter, brown sugar and cinnamon in a bowl. Layer the frozen rolls, pudding mix, nuts and cherries or raisins in a greased and floured bundt pan. Drizzle the butter mixture over the top. Cover with a paper towel. Let rise for 8 to 12 hours. Bake, uncovered, at 350 degrees for 25 minutes or until golden brown.

Serves 12

Monkey Bread

4 (8-ounce) cans biscuits
2/3 cup sugar
1/2 tablespoon cinnamon
3/4 cup (1 1/2 sticks) butter or
   margarine
1 cup sugar
1 tablespoon cinnamon
1/2 cup chopped pecans
   (optional)
1/2 cup raisins (optional)

Separate the biscuits. Cut each into quarters using kitchen shears. Mix 2/3 cup sugar and 1/2 tablespoon cinnamon in a large sealable plastic food storage bag. Add the biscuit dough quarters and seal the bag. Toss until each piece is well coated. Bring the butter, 1 cup sugar and 1 tablespoon cinnamon to a boil in a medium saucepan over medium-high heat. Alternate layers of the biscuit pieces, sugar mixture, pecans and raisins in a greased bundt pan until all ingredients are used. Bake at 350 degrees for 30 to 35 minutes or until golden brown. Cool in the pan for 10 minutes. Invert onto a serving plate. Let family or guests serve themselves by simply pulling apart the bread.

Serves 8

Macadamia Nut French Toast

4 eggs, lightly beaten
1/4 cup sugar
1/4 teaspoon ground nutmeg
2/3 cup orange juice
1/3 cup milk
1/2 teaspoon vanilla extract
1 (16-ounce) loaf Italian bread,
    cut into 1-inch slices

2/3 cup butter, melted
1/2 cup macadamia nuts, chopped,
    toasted
Garnishes: Confectioners' sugar,
    ground nutmeg

Combine the eggs, sugar, 1/4 teaspoon nutmeg, orange juice, milk and vanilla in a mixing bowl and beat well. Arrange the bread slices in a single layer in a lightly greased 9×13-inch baking dish. Pour the egg mixture over the top. Chill, covered, for 8 hours or longer, turning the bread once.

Pour the butter into a 10×15-inch baking pan. Arrange the bread slices in a single layer in the butter. Bake at 400 degrees for 10 minutes. Sprinkle with the macadamia nuts. Bake for 10 minutes longer. Garnish with confectioners' sugar and nutmeg. Serve immediately with maple syrup.

Serves 6

Pain Perdu (French Toast)

1 egg
1 teaspoon vanilla extract
2 tablespoons sugar
1 cup milk
1/2 teaspoon cinnamon

1/4 teaspoon salt
1/2 cup (1 stick) butter or margarine
6 slices white, wheat or
    pumpernickel bread

Beat the egg, vanilla, sugar, milk, cinnamon and salt in a medium mixing bowl. Melt the butter in a large skillet over medium heat. Dip the bread slices in the egg mixture until soaked through. Place in the skillet in a single layer. Cook on both sides until golden brown. Serve with your favorite syrup.

Serves 6

Ham and Cheese Rolls

2 (8-ounce) packages miniature dinner rolls (1×3 inches)
8 ounces sliced ham
8 ounces sliced Swiss cheese
$1/4$ cup ($1/2$ stick) butter or margarine, melted
$1/2$ teaspoon Worcestershire sauce
$1^1/2$ tablespoons honey
$1^1/2$ tablespoons mustard
$1^1/2$ tablespoons poppy seeds

Remove the rolls in a single layer from each foil pan. Cut each layer horizontally into halves using an electric knife. Return the bottom layers to the foil pans or place in 9×13-inch baking pans. Layer the ham and Swiss cheese over the bottom layers. Replace the top bread layers. Combine the butter, Worcestershire sauce, honey, mustard and poppy seeds in a bowl and blend well. Brush over the roll tops. Cover with foil. Bake at 350 degrees for 15 minutes. Remove from the pans to a cutting board. Cut along the perforations with an electric knife.

Serves 20

Note: This is a great way to use leftover holiday ham.

Ham and Asparagus Brunch Bake

2 (6-ounce) packages original recipe long grain and wild rice
1 pound asparagus, cut into pieces
2 cups chopped ham
1 cup chopped red bell pepper
$1/4$ cup finely chopped red onion
1 cup shredded sharp Cheddar cheese

Prepare the rice in a saucepan using the package directions, adding the asparagus during the last 5 minutes of cooking. Remove the saucepan from the heat. Add the ham, bell pepper and onion and mix well. Spoon into a greased $7^1/2$×11-inch baking dish. Sprinkle with the cheese. Bake at 350 degrees for 25 to 30 minutes or until heated through.

Serves 6

Breakfast Casserole

1 pound ground sausage
4 slices white bread, cubed
6 eggs
2 cups milk

1 teaspoon dry mustard
Salt and pepper to taste
1 cup grated Cheddar cheese
1 cup grated Swiss cheese

Brown the sausage in a skillet, stirring until crumbly; drain. Layer the bread cubes in a buttered 9×13-inch baking dish. Beat the eggs in a mixing bowl. Stir in the milk, dry mustard, salt and pepper. Add the sausage, Cheddar cheese and Swiss cheese and mix well. Pour over the bread cubes. Bake at 325 degrees for 35 minutes.

Serves 12

Note: You may assemble ahead and chill, covered, for 8 to 12 hours before baking.

Variations: Don't be afraid to experiment with this one—the recipe works just as well with ham or bacon substituted for the sausage, and your favorite cheese can be substituted for one or both of the above.

Apple Sausage Quiche

8 ounces ground sausage
1/2 cup mayonnaise
2 tablespoons flour
1/2 cup milk
2 eggs
1 green apple, such as a Granny
   Smith, peeled, sliced

1 cup shredded Swiss cheese
1 cup shredded Monterey Jack
   cheese
1 unbaked (10-inch) deep-dish
   pie shell

Brown the sausage in a skillet over medium heat, stirring until crumbly; drain. Mix the mayonnaise and flour in a bowl. Whisk in the milk and eggs until blended. Toss the apple, Swiss cheese, Monterey Jack cheese and sausage in a bowl. Spoon the sausage mixture into the pie shell. Pour the egg mixture over the top. Bake at 350 degrees for 1 hour.

Serves 6

Variations: Try substituting ham or bacon for the sausage and spinach or mushrooms for the apple.

Vidalia Onion Pie

3 cups chopped Vidalia onions
3 tablespoons butter or margarine
1 cup cottage cheese
1 cup sour cream
1 cup shredded Cheddar cheese
3 eggs, beaten
2 tablespoons milk
1 tablespoon self-rising flour
1 teaspoon sugar
1 unbaked (9-inch) pie shell

Sauté the onions in the butter in a skillet until transparent. Remove from the heat. Add the cottage cheese, sour cream, Cheddar cheese, eggs, milk, flour and sugar and mix well. Spoon into the pie shell. Bake at 350 degrees for 45 to 60 minutes or until set. Cool for 10 to 15 minutes before serving.

Serves 6

Garlic Cheese Grits

4 cups water
1/2 teaspoon salt
1 cup uncooked regular grits
1 garlic clove, minced
8 ounces Velveeta cheese, cubed
1/4 cup half-and-half
2 tablespoons butter

Bring the water and salt to a boil in a large saucepan. Stir in the grits and garlic gradually. Cover and reduce the heat. Cook for 10 minutes, stirring occasionally. Add the cheese, half-and-half and butter. Simmer until the cheese and butter melt, stirring constantly.

Serves 6

Christmas Brunch Traditions

Borrow these ideas from our members:

* We have a big breakfast at midnight on Christmas Eve. Who can sleep through that night, anyway?
* We have an open-house brunch on Christmas Day so all the neighborhood children can play together. Everyone brings a dish.
* We open one gift on Christmas Eve to ease the tension and get the kids to sleep. The next morning, Dad fixes breakfast!
* We have the same Holiday Casserole and side dishes every year.
* On such a topsy-turvy day, eating breakfast at night makes perfect sense for us.

Borrow these brunch traditions from our members.

City of Norcross

Norcross was founded in 1870 as a resort town for wealthy Atlantans. Visitors would arrive by train at the Norcross depot, located at the center of the city and across from Thrasher Park, and stay at the Brunswick luxury hotel. Founder J. J. Thrasher named the city for his good friend and former mayor of Atlanta, Jonathan Norcross. Norcross is Gwinnett's second-oldest city and is distinguished as the only location in Gwinnett County having a district on the U.S. Register of Historic Places. Enjoying a population boom in the 1980s, Norcross now has a population of 6,000 in its 3.8-square-mile area.

The city of Norcross prides itself in maintaining its quiet, small town appeal while being amidst high-quality, high-tech commercial industry in areas like Technology Park. The southern pines, scattered oaks, and network of sidewalks connecting the city's several parks to the central historic district lend picturesque character and the relaxed atmosphere of a bygone era.

Soups

Seafood Bisque

1 (10-ounce) can tomato soup
1 (11-ounce) can pea soup
1 (10-ounce) can cream of mushroom soup
1 (10-ounce) can golden mushroom soup
1 (10-ounce) can consommé
2 cups half-and-half
6 green onions, chopped
$1/4$ cup chopped parsley
1 teaspoon basil
Tabasco sauce to taste
$1/2$ cup sliced mushrooms
$1/4$ cup dry white wine or vermouth
1 (6-ounce) can shrimp, rinsed, drained
1 (7-ounce) can crab meat, drained

Combine the tomato soup, pea soup, cream of mushroom soup, golden mushroom soup, consommé, half-and-half, green onions, parsley, basil, Tabasco sauce, mushrooms, wine, shrimp and crab meat in a large stockpot. Bring to a boil and reduce the heat. Simmer until heated through, stirring frequently.

Serves 8

Variation: Double the recipe and substitute 1 pound crawfish tails and 1 pound of fresh crab meat for the canned shrimp and crab meat.

Potato and Corn Chowder

3 tablespoons butter
1 small onion, chopped
2 garlic cloves, minced
$^1/_2$ cup chopped celery
$^1/_2$ cup chopped carrot
2 (14-ounce) cans chicken broth
4 cups chopped peeled potatoes
$^1/_2$ teaspoon salt
1 teaspoon pepper
3 cups half-and-half
4 cups fresh or frozen corn kernels
Garnishes: Bacon bits and chopped green onions

Melt the butter in a Dutch oven. Add the onion, garlic, celery and carrot and sauté until tender. Stir in the chicken broth, potatoes, salt and pepper. Bring to a boil and reduce the heat. Simmer for 30 to 45 minutes or until the potatoes are tender. Stir in the half-and-half and corn. Cook for 25 to 30 minutes or until of the desired consistency, stirring frequently. Ladle into soup bowls. Garnish with bacon bits and chopped green onions.

Makes 2$^1/_2$ quarts

From the Wine List

It's a rare wintry, cold night in the South. You've got a big fire going, a hearty soup or stew warming on the stove, and a chunk of corn bread for dunking. What kind of wine goes with all of the above? Try a wine that will balance the intense tomato taste of chili, gazpacho, and other vine-ripe soups. A white bordeaux from France will balance all that flavor with a light, crisp, clean, and dry taste. Another white wine alternative is pinot grigio, a grape variety from Italy that produces an aroma with citrus and floral notes. Whatever your wine preference, keep it simple tonight and dine on trays in front of the fire.

Another white wine alternative is pinot grigio, a grape variety from Italy that produces an aroma with citrus and floral notes.

Gazpacho

6 tablespoons olive oil
1/4 cup red wine vinegar
1/4 teaspoon salt
1 teaspoon garlic, minced
4 (1-ounce) hard rolls, torn, or
  4 ounces crusty French bread, torn
1 green bell pepper, seeded, chopped
1 medium cucumber, peeled, seeded,
  chopped

1/4 cup chopped red onion
2 cups chopped seeded tomatoes
1 cup water
1/2 teaspoon cumin
1/4 teaspoon white pepper
Garnishes: Sour cream, chopped
  cucumbers

Blend the olive oil, red wine vinegar, salt and garlic in a large bowl. Add
the rolls, bell pepper, 1 cucumber, red onion, tomatoes, water, cumin and white
pepper and mix well. Chill, covered, for 8 to 12 hours. Process in a food
processor until nearly smooth. Pour into soup bowls. Garnish with sour cream
and chopped cucumbers.

Serves 6

Asparagus Soup

1 pound asparagus, cut up
3 scallions with tops, sliced
12 ounces mushrooms, sliced
2 tablespoons butter
3 tablespoons flour
6 tablespoons butter, melted

1/2 teaspoon salt
1/4 teaspoon pepper
2 cups chicken broth
1 (11-ounce) can white Shoe Peg
  corn
2 cups light cream

Sauté the asparagus, scallions and mushrooms in 2 tablespoons butter in a skillet
until the asparagus is tender. Mix the flour, 6 tablespoons butter, salt and pepper
in a bowl. Add some of the chicken broth and blend until smooth. Add the flour
mixture, corn, remaining broth and cream to the sautéed vegetables. Cook until
heated through.

Serves 6

French Onion Soup

4 large onions, thinly sliced, separated
1/2 cup (1 stick) butter or margarine
1 tablespoon flour
1 (15-ounce) can chicken broth
1 (15-ounce) can beef broth
2 cups water
1/4 cup dry white wine
Pepper to taste
8 slices French bread
3 slices mozzarella cheese, cut up
1/2 cup grated Parmesan cheese

Sauté the onions in the butter in a skillet until tender. Add the flour and stir until blended and smooth. Add the chicken broth, beef broth, water and wine gradually, stirring constantly. Bring to a boil and reduce the heat. Simmer for 15 minutes. Season with pepper. Ladle the soup into ovenproof bowls. Place the French bread over the top of the soup. Sprinkle with the mozzarella cheese and Parmesan cheese. Broil until the cheese melts.

Serves 8

Potato Soup

2 ribs celery, chopped
1 medium onion, chopped
2 tablespoons butter
6 medium potatoes, peeled, cubed
2 carrots, chopped
3 cups water
5 chicken bouillon cubes
$^3/_4$ teaspoon seasoned salt
$^1/_2$ teaspoon thyme
Dash of garlic powder
Dash of pepper
2 cups milk
1 cup shredded Cheddar or Swiss cheese

Sauté the celery and onion in the butter in a skillet until tender. Add the potatoes, carrots, water, bouillon cubes, seasoned salt, thyme, garlic powder and pepper. Simmer, covered, for 20 minutes or until the potatoes are tender. Remove from the heat. Mash the vegetables with a potato masher. Add the milk and cheese. Cook until the cheese melts, stirring constantly.

Serves 6

Curried Acorn Squash Soup

3 medium acorn squash, cut into halves, seeded
1/2 cup chopped onion
3 to 4 teaspoons curry powder
2 tablespoons butter or margarine
3 cups chicken broth
1 cup half-and-half
1/2 teaspoon ground nutmeg
Salt and pepper to taste
Garnish: Crumbled cooked bacon

Place the squash cut side down in a greased shallow baking pan. Bake
at 350 degrees for 35 to 40 minutes or until the squash is almost tender.
Sauté the onion and curry powder in the butter in a skillet over medium
heat until the onion is tender. Remove from the heat. Scoop out the
squash pulp and add to the saucepan, discarding the shell. Add the
chicken broth gradually, stirring constantly. Cook over medium heat
for 15 to 20 minutes or until the squash is tender. Process the squash
mixture in a food processor or blender until smooth. Return to the
saucepan. Stir in the half-and-half, nutmeg, salt and pepper. Cook
over low heat until heated through; do not boil. Ladle into soup bowls.
Garnish with crumbled bacon.

Serves 4 to 6

Tortilla Soup

6 tablespoons vegetable oil
8 corn tortillas, chopped
6 garlic cloves, minced
1/2 cup fresh cilantro, chopped
1 medium onion, chopped
1 (28-ounce) can diced tomatoes
2 tablespoons cumin
1 tablespoon chili powder
3 bay leaves
6 cups chicken broth
1 teaspoon salt
1/2 teaspoon cayenne pepper
4 to 6 chicken breasts, cooked, shredded or cubed
Garnishes: Shredded Monterey Jack cheese, cubed peeled avocado,
    sour cream, 2 corn tortillas, sliced, crisp-fried

Heat the oil in a large saucepan over medium heat. Add the chopped corn
tortillas, garlic, cilantro and onion. Sauté for 2 to 3 minutes or until the onion
is transparent. Stir in the tomatoes. Bring to a boil. Add the cumin, chili
powder, bay leaves and chicken broth. Return to a boil and reduce the heat.
Add the salt and cayenne pepper. Simmer for 30 minutes. Remove the bay
leaves. Stir in the chicken. Simmer until the chicken is heated through. Ladle
into soup bowls. Garnish with Monterey Jack cheese, avocado, sour cream and
crisp-fried corn tortillas.

Serves 6

Tomato Basil Soup

10 to 12 Roma tomatoes, peeled, or
   1 (28-ounce) can whole tomatoes, drained
3 cups tomato juice
2 cups chicken stock
15 (or more) fresh basil leaves
1½ cups heavy cream
¾ cup (1½ sticks) unsalted butter, cut into pieces
½ teaspoon salt
½ teaspoon freshly ground pepper
Garnish: Freshly grated Parmesan cheese

Combine the tomatoes, tomato juice and chicken stock in a large saucepan. Simmer for 30 minutes. Add the basil and mix well. Process the soup in batches in a food processor or blender until smooth. Return to the saucepan. Whisk in the cream, butter, salt and pepper. Cook over low heat until the butter melts and the soup is heated through, whisking constantly. Ladle into soup bowls. Garnish with Parmesan cheese.

Serves 8 to 10

Cowboy Stew

1 pound ground beef
1/2 cup chopped onion
1 (10-ounce) can tomatoes with green chiles
1 (14-ounce) can stewed tomatoes
1 (15-ounce) can cream-style corn
1 (16-ounce) can mixed vegetables, drained
1 (13-ounce) can Spanish rice

Brown the ground beef with the onion in a skillet, stirring until the ground beef is crumbly; drain. Add the tomatoes with green chiles, stewed tomatoes, corn, mixed vegetables and Spanish rice and mix well. Simmer for 1 hour. Serve with corn bread muffins.

Serves 6

Vegetarian Skillet Chili

2 tablespoons olive oil
1 cup chopped onion
2 teaspoons chili powder
1 teaspoon cumin
2 (10-ounce) cans tomatoes with green chiles
1 large sweet potato, peeled, chopped
1 large zucchini, sliced
2 (16-ounce) cans black beans, rinsed, drained

Heat the olive oil in a 12-inch skillet. Add the onion. Sauté until brown. Stir in the chili powder and cumin. Add the tomatoes with green chiles and sweet potato. Cover and reduce the heat. Simmer for 6 minutes or until the sweet potato is partially cooked through. Add the zucchini. Cook until the zucchini is steamed. Add the black beans. Cook until heated through.

Serves 4

Bodacious Chili

2 pounds boneless beef chuck
   roast, cut into 1-inch cubes
2 large onions, chopped
3 ribs celery, sliced
1 each large green and red bell
   pepper, coarsely chopped
1 cup sliced fresh mushrooms
2 jalapeño chiles, seeded,
   chopped
4 garlic cloves, minced
3 tablespoons olive oil
1/2 cup burgundy
1 tablespoon molasses
2 tablespoons baking cocoa

2 tablespoons chili powder
1 teaspoon each cumin, oregano,
   paprika and turmeric
1/2 teaspoon salt
1/2 teaspoon cardamom
1/4 teaspoon pepper
2 (16-ounce) cans whole
   tomatoes, drained, chopped
1 (16-ounce) can kidney beans,
   drained
1 (16-ounce) can chick-peas,
   drained
Shredded Cheddar cheese
Spicy Sour Cream Topping (below)

Cook the beef, onions, celery, bell peppers, mushrooms, jalapeño chiles and garlic in the olive oil in a large Dutch oven over medium-high heat until the beef is brown, stirring constantly; drain. Add the wine, molasses, baking cocoa and seasonings and mix well. Stir in the tomatoes, kidney beans and chick-peas. Bring to a boil. Cover and reduce the heat. Simmer for 1 1/2 hours, stirring occasionally. Serve with Cheddar cheese and Spicy Sour Cream Topping.

Serves 6 to 8

Spicy Sour Cream Topping

1 cup sour cream
1/3 cup salsa
2 tablespoons mayonnaise
1 tablespoon lemon juice
1 teaspoon Dijon mustard

1 teaspoon chili powder
1/2 teaspoon onion powder
1/2 teaspoon curry powder
Dash of ground red pepper

Combine all the ingredients in a bowl and mix well. Chill, covered, until ready to serve.

Makes 1 3/4 cups

The Art of Chili

Every die-hard cook worth his or her hot sauce has a prize-worthy chili recipe with their own "secret something." If your repertoire is lacking in the chili department, start with this "bodacious" recipe and add or delete ingredients to your heart's content. Top off your creativity with this Spicy Sour Cream Topping.

If your repertoire is lacking in the chili department, start with this "bodacious" recipe and add or delete ingredients to your heart's content.

Southwest White Chili

1 teaspoon olive oil
1¹/₂ pounds boneless skinless chicken breasts, cut into
   small pieces
¹/₄ cup chopped onion
1 cup chicken broth
1 (4-ounce) can chopped green chiles
1 teaspoon garlic powder
1 teaspoon ground cumin
¹/₂ teaspoon oregano
¹/₂ teaspoon cilantro
¹/₈ teaspoon ground red pepper
1 (9-ounce) can white kidney beans (cannellini)
Garnishes: 2 green onions, sliced, 1 cup shredded cheese

Heat the olive oil in a large saucepan over medium-high heat. Add the chicken and onion. Cook for 4 to 5 minutes or until the chicken is cooked through. Stir in the chicken broth, green chiles, garlic powder, cumin, oregano, cilantro and red pepper. Simmer for 15 minutes. Stir in the undrained beans. Simmer for 5 minutes. Ladle into soup bowls. Garnish with the green onions and cheese.

Serves 4 to 6

Park Ranger Jerry's Chili

1 pound ground beef
1 small onion, chopped
2 ribs celery, chopped
1 garlic clove, minced
1 (16-ounce) can hot chili beans
1/2 cup ketchup
2 cups water

1 teaspoon salt
1/2 teaspoon black pepper
1/2 teaspoon sugar
1/2 teaspoon chili powder
1/4 teaspoon red pepper or hot
  pepper sauce

Brown the ground beef in a large Dutch oven over medium heat, stirring until crumbly; drain. Add the onion, celery, garlic, chili beans, ketchup, water, salt, black pepper, sugar, chili powder and red pepper and mix well. Cook over medium heat until bubbly, stirring occasionally. Reduce the heat to low. Simmer until ready to serve.

Serves 6

Chicken Chili

1 small onion, chopped
1 green bell pepper, seeded,
  chopped
2 tablespoons butter or
  margarine
1 pound chicken, cooked,
  shredded
2 (15-ounce) cans diced
  tomatoes

1 (15-ounce) can Great
  Northern beans, drained
1 (15-ounce) can pinto beans,
  drained
1 cup salsa
1 to 3 tablespoons chili powder
Salt and pepper to taste

Sauté the onion and bell pepper in the butter in a skillet until tender. Combine with the chicken, tomatoes, Great Northern beans, pinto beans and salsa in a slow cooker. Cook on Low for 3 to 4 hours. Add the chili powder, salt and pepper. Serve with a salad and bread for a great dinner.

Serves 4 to 6

Take a Walk on the Wild Side!

Sometimes our community service takes us into the wild. The Owl Prowl and Frog Frolics are a sample of the family outings that help support Geosphere, a unique National Park setting along the Chattahoochee River bordering Gwinnett and North Fulton counties. At one of these events, you might find a pot of this chili cooking as Park Ranger Jerry Hightower shares this wonderful park with guests. Park Ranger Hightower oversees this environmental education program for teachers and students in our community.

Roswell

Originally a small southern mill town, Roswell now boasts a population of 55,000 and was recently voted a "Top 10" living community. The town prides itself on being economically strong and rich in history. Roswell is located in North Fulton County on the banks of Vickery Creek, a tributary of the Chattahoochee River. In 1828, the area attracted Roswell King and inspired him to build a dam and a mill and create what was to become one of the most important manufacturing towns in the state of Georgia.

The mills of Roswell supplying Confederate troops with the famous "Roswell Gray" woolens, in addition to an important bridge over the Chattahoochee River, caused the area to become a target for Federal troops during the Civil War. Even though Sherman burned much of the town on his March to the Sea, several classic Greek Revival homes survived the war and can be visited today.

Modern Roswell boasts a beautiful town square that hosts outdoor concerts and art festivals. Commerce is centered in the many office complexes around the Georgia Highway 400 area instead of the mills. The heart of Roswell can be seen in its many charities and civic organizations, one of which is North Fulton Community Charities, a multifaceted organization that helps many families in need.

Salads

Sweet and Crunchy Garden Salad

1 head iceberg lettuce, rinsed
1 head romaine, rinsed
1 cup sliced or slivered almonds
1/4 cup sugar
1 cup vegetable oil
1/4 cup vinegar
1/4 cup sugar

1 tablespoon parsley flakes
1 teaspoon salt
Dash of black pepper
Dash of red pepper
6 green onion tops, thinly sliced
1 (22-ounce) can mandarin oranges,
    drained, chilled

Tear the iceberg lettuce and romaine into bite-size pieces into a bowl. Chill, covered, in the refrigerator. Combine the almonds and 1/4 cup sugar in a saucepan. Cook over medium heat until the sugar browns, stirring constantly. Spread on an ungreased baking sheet. Let stand until cool. Break into tiny pieces. Combine the oil, vinegar, 1/4 cup sugar, parsley flakes, salt, black pepper and red pepper in a bowl and mix well. Chill, covered, in the refrigerator. Combine the lettuce mixture, green onions, caramelized almonds and mandarin oranges in a large salad bowl and toss to mix. Add the desired amount of dressing and toss to coat.

Serves 10

"Dig Deep" Salad

1 head lettuce, rinsed
2 onions, thinly sliced into rings
1/2 cup minced green bell pepper
1 (8-ounce) can water chestnuts,
    drained, chopped
1 (10-ounce) package frozen green
    peas, thawed

2 cups mayonnaise
1/4 to 1/2 cup grated Romano cheese
2 hard-cooked eggs, sliced
12 cherry tomatoes
2 tablespoons bacon bits

Tear the lettuce into bite-size pieces. Layer the lettuce, onion rings, bell pepper, water chestnuts and uncooked green peas in a trifle bowl. Spread the mayonnaise over the top, sealing to the edge. Sprinkle with Romano cheese. Chill, covered, for 24 hours. Layer the eggs, tomatoes and bacon bits over the top. Be sure your guests "dig deep" to get some of everything.

Serves 8

Crisp Mixed Greens with Apple and Warm Brie

1 Red or Golden Delicious apple, thinly sliced
Apple juice or cider
4 thick-cut slices bacon
1/4 cup apple juice or cider
1/4 cup balsamic vinegar
1 tablespoon brown sugar
8 ounces round Brie cheese
2 tablespoons brown sugar
1/4 cup chopped walnuts or pecans
6 cups mixed salad greens

Dip the apple slices into some apple juice or cider in a bowl to prevent browning. Cook the bacon in a skillet until crisp. Remove to paper towels to drain. Crumble the bacon. Drain the skillet, reserving 2 tablespoons bacon drippings. Add 1/4 cup apple juice, balsamic vinegar and 1 tablespoon brown sugar to the reserved bacon drippings in the skillet. Heat until the brown sugar dissolves, stirring constantly. Place the Brie cheese on a baking sheet and cut into 6 wedges. Sprinkle with 2 tablespoons brown sugar and walnuts. Bake at 450 degrees for 2 to 3 minutes.

To serve, divide the salad greens among 6 serving plates. Arrange the apple slices and a wedge of Brie cheese on each plate. Drizzle with the salad dressing and sprinkle with the crumbled bacon.

Serves 6

Easy Salad Samplers

It's summertime in the South and time to take a break from the heat! Keep your kitchen cool and forget turning on the oven tonight. Look to our salads for the perfect solution when time and tempers are short and appetites are long and hungry. Just a few ingredients from the refrigerator and pantry and you've got the makings for a great supper salad with make-ahead convenience. Add any of these to customize our salads or use in combination to create one of your own.

** Cubed cooked chicken
(1 cup per person)
* Cubed cooked turkey or
ham (1 cup per person)
* Cooked peeled shrimp
* Cooked pasta
* Crumbled cooked bacon
* Shredded cheese
* Chopped hard-cooked eggs
* Sliced or chopped
vegetables
* Fruits in season*

Dijon Spinach Salad

1 pound fresh spinach, torn
6 slices bacon, cooked, crumbled
2 hard-cooked eggs, chopped
1 cup fresh mushrooms, sliced
$1/4$ cup vegetable oil
$1/4$ cup olive oil

2 tablespoons lemon juice
1 tablespoon white wine vinegar
$1/2$ teaspoon Dijon mustard
$1/4$ teaspoon salt
$1/4$ teaspoon pepper

Combine the spinach, bacon, hard-cooked eggs and mushrooms in a large salad bowl and toss gently to mix. Combine the vegetable oil, olive oil, lemon juice, white wine vinegar, Dijon mustard, salt and pepper in a jar with a tight-fitting lid. Cover tightly and shake to blend. Pour over the spinach mixture and toss gently to coat.

Serves 6

Strawberry Pecan Spinach Salad

$1/2$ cup pecan halves
1 pound baby spinach
1 pint strawberries, hulled, cut into
   halves
$1^1/2$ tablespoons poppy seeds
1 cup light vegetable oil

$1/3$ cup red wine vinegar
2 tablespoons finely chopped onions
$1/4$ cup sugar
1 teaspoon salt
1 teaspoon dry mustard

Spread the pecans in a single layer on a baking sheet. Bake at 350 degrees for 8 to 10 minutes or until toasted. Combine the spinach, strawberries, pecans and poppy seeds in a large salad bowl. Combine the vegetable oil, red wine vinegar, onions, sugar, salt and dry mustard in a small bowl and whisk well to blend. Pour the desired amount of the dressing over the spinach mixture and toss to coat.

Serves 4

Fabulous Cold Bean Salad

1 (14-ounce) can French-style green beans, drained
1 (15-ounce) can black beans, drained
1 (14-ounce) can young green peas, drained
1 (14-ounce) can white whole kernel corn, drained
1 medium sweet onion, chopped
$^1/_2$ yellow bell pepper, chopped
$^1/_2$ red bell pepper, chopped
1 (2-ounce) jar pimentos, drained
$^1/_2$ cup vegetable oil
$^1/_2$ cup vinegar
$^3/_4$ cup sugar
1 teaspoon salt

Combine the green beans, black beans, green peas and corn in a bowl.
Add the onion, bell peppers and pimentos and toss to mix well. Combine
the oil, vinegar, sugar and salt in a small bowl. Beat with a whisk for
4 minutes. Pour over the vegetables and toss to coat. Marinate, covered,
in the refrigerator for 8 to 12 hours before serving.

Serves 8 to 10

Green Bean and Tomato Salad

3 pounds green beans, trimmed, cut
   into 2-inch pieces
Salt to taste
2 pints cherry tomatoes, halved, or
   whole grape tomatoes
3 tablespoons country-style Dijon
   mustard

$1/4$ cup sherry wine vinegar
$2/3$ cup olive oil
$1/3$ cup minced shallots
Pepper to taste

Cook the green beans in boiling salted water in a large saucepan for 5 minutes
or until tender-crisp; drain. Rinse under cold running water and drain well.
Combine the green beans and tomatoes in a large salad bowl. Mix the Dijon
mustard and wine vinegar in a small bowl. Add the olive oil gradually, whisking
constantly. Add the shallots and mix well. Pour over the green bean mixture
and toss to coat. Season with salt and pepper to taste.

Serves 12

*Note: You may prepare the salad one day in advance by placing the cooked cooled green beans in a
sealable plastic food storage bag and storing in the refrigerator. Prepare the dressing and let stand
at room temperature.*

Broccoli Salad

2 heads broccoli
1 medium red onion
8 slices bacon
1 cup mayonnaise

$1/2$ cup sugar
3 tablespoons red wine vinegar
$1/2$ cup raisins
1 cup pecans, chopped

Cut the broccoli florets into bite-size pieces. Peel the broccoli stems and cut
into thin strips. Cut the onion into thin slices and separate into rings. Cook
the bacon in a skillet until crisp; drain. Crumble the bacon. Combine the
mayonnaise, sugar and red wine vinegar in a small bowl and mix well.

To assemble, combine the broccoli, onion rings, bacon, raisins and pecans in a
large salad bowl. Add the dressing and toss gently to evenly coat. Chill, covered,
until ready to serve.

Serves 8

Napa Salad

1 (3-ounce) package ramen noodles
6 cups napa cabbage or Chinese cabbage (bok choy), chopped
3 green onions, chopped
1 small package sliced almonds, toasted
2 tablespoons sesame seeds
1/2 cup vegetable oil
6 tablespoons rice vinegar
1 tablespoon sugar
Salt and pepper to taste

Crumble the ramen noodles, reserving the seasoning packet for the dressing. Combine the cabbage, green onions, almonds, sesame seeds and ramen noodles in a bowl and toss to mix well. Mix the oil, rice vinegar, sugar, reserved seasoning, salt and pepper in a bowl. Pour over the cabbage mixture and toss to coat. Chill, covered, in the refrigerator until ready to serve.

Serves 6

Variations: Stir in 3 cups chopped cooked chicken for a heartier meal. Stir in one 8-ounce can of mandarin oranges, drained, for a citrus flair.

Enjoy a Potluck Potpourri

Covered dish dinners are a great southern tradition, and all the recipes featured in this section travel well. Why not make your next get-together a taste-testing feast, and ask friends to bring their favorite covered dish? You supply the salads, drinks, and appetizers, and voila, you've got a potluck party!

A potluck party is a great idea for a second baby shower. For the mother-to-be who already has all the baby necessities, nothing is more welcome than a break from cooking. When planning the shower, tell guests to include copies of the recipes with their casserole, and make sure it's a dish that freezes well.

When preparing a covered dish to take to a potluck event, don't assume there will be either time or room in your hostess' kitchen for final preparations when you arrive. Plan to bring a dish that is ready to go "as is." With everyone sharing the work, a potluck menu is a fun and easy way to entertain or be entertained.

71

Creamy Coleslaw

1 medium head green cabbage
1 large carrot
$^{1}/_{2}$ cup finely chopped sweet onion
2 tablespoons sweet pickle juice
1 teaspoon sugar
$^{2}/_{3}$ cup mayonnaise
Salt and pepper to taste

Process the cabbage and carrot in a blender or food processor until chopped. Pour into a large bowl. Add the onion, pickle juice, sugar, mayonnaise, salt and pepper and mix well.

Serves 12

Marinated Potato Salad

2 pounds new red potatoes
1 small red onion, thinly sliced
$^{1}/_{2}$ cup olive oil
$^{1}/_{4}$ cup vegetable oil
$^{1}/_{4}$ cup red wine vinegar
2 tablespoons Dijon mustard
1 teaspoon dried basil, or 4 fresh basil leaves, chopped
$^{1}/_{2}$ teaspoon salt
$^{1}/_{4}$ teaspoon white pepper

Cook the potatoes in enough boiling water to cover in a Dutch oven for 8 minutes or until tender; drain. Cool and cut into thin slices. Place the potatoes and onion in a large bowl. Combine the olive oil, vegetable oil, red wine vinegar, Dijon mustard, basil, salt and white pepper in a small bowl and mix well. Pour over the potato mixture. Marinate, covered, in the refrigerator for 8 hours, stirring occasionally.

Serves 10

Creamy Roasted Potato Salad

3 pounds small new potatoes, cut into eighths
2 onions, cut into quarters
6 garlic cloves, minced
$1/4$ cup olive oil
$1/2$ cup mayonnaise
$1/2$ cup sour cream
$1/4$ cup lemon juice
3 tablespoons chopped fresh chives
$1/4$ cup fresh parsley, chopped
2 tablespoons capers, drained
1 teaspoon salt
1 teaspoon pepper

Combine the potatoes, onions, garlic and olive oil in a bowl and toss
to coat. Place in a 10×15-inch baking pan. Roast at 400 degrees for
30 to 40 minutes or until tender and brown, stirring once; drain and
cool. Combine the mayonnaise, sour cream, lemon juice, chives, parsley,
capers, salt and pepper in a large serving bowl. Add the potato mixture
and toss gently to coat. Chill, covered, until ready to serve.

Serves 12

Black-Eyed Pea Salad

2 (15-ounce) cans black-eyed peas,
   rinsed, drained
1 medium onion, chopped
1 garlic clove, pressed
2 tomatoes, chopped
3 ribs celery, chopped

$^1/_2$ cup sliced mushrooms
1 (4-ounce) can sliced black olives
1 (8-ounce) bottle zesty Italian salad
   dressing
1$^1/_2$ teaspoons oregano
Salt and pepper to taste

Combine the black-eyed peas, onion, garlic, tomatoes, celery, mushrooms and
olives in a large bowl and mix well. Add the Italian salad dressing, oregano,
salt and pepper and toss to coat. Marinate, covered, in the refrigerator for 8 to
12 hours. Drain before serving.

Serves 8 to 10

Southern Chicken Salad

3 cups chopped cooked chicken breasts
$^1/_4$ cup chopped celery
$^1/_4$ cup chopped onion
$^1/_4$ cup sweet pickle cubes
$^1/_2$ cup (or more) mayonnaise
Salt and pepper to taste
Garnish: $^1/_2$ cup chopped pecans

Combine the chicken, celery, onion, pickle cubes, mayonnaise, salt and pepper
in a bowl and stir gently to mix. Add more mayonnaise if needed for the desired
consistency. Chill, covered, until ready to serve. Garnish with chopped pecans
just before serving.

Serves 6

Taco Salad

1 large head lettuce, rinsed
2 or 3 fresh tomatoes, chopped
1 large onion, chopped
1 (4-ounce) can sliced black olives, drained
1 pound ground beef
1 envelope taco seasoning mix
6 ounces Cheddar cheese, shredded
1 medium package regular tortilla chips, broken into bite-size pieces
1 (8-ounce) bottle creamy Italian or ranch salad dressing

Tear the lettuce into bite-size pieces and place in a salad bowl. Add the tomatoes, onion and olives. Chill, covered, in the refrigerator. Brown the ground beef in a large skillet over medium-high heat, stirring until crumbly, drain. Add the taco seasoning mix and prepare using the package directions.

To serve, add the hot ground beef mixture to the chilled salad. Add the Cheddar cheese, tortilla chips and salad dressing and toss until mixed. Serve immediately.

Serves 4

Swinging a Mallet on the Greensward

Croquet, anyone? In 1989, the League introduced one of its first major fund-raisers, "A Day of Croquet." Attendees wore their finest summer whites and had a day of civilized fun outside.

In its first year, the event netted $23,000 to benefit child abuse prevention programs in Gwinnett and North Fulton counties. League members created a fun picnic setting—box lunches, pony rides and wicket shots for children, and a silent auction. In the evening, the 106 competitors danced under the stars at a Black Tie and Sneakers Ball.

Plan your own informal Day of Croquet for the next family reunion or weekend gathering. Buy an inexpensive croquet set, and challenge the family to a match. Early spring is the perfect time to dress up, as well as to serve up some fresh, cool salads like the ones in this chapter.

Shrimp Pasta Salad

2 pounds small shrimp
1 bay leaf
1 lemon, sliced
16 ounces uncooked ruffled pasta
3 green onions, chopped
1 green bell pepper, seeded, chopped
1 red bell pepper, seeded, chopped
1 yellow bell pepper, seeded, chopped
1 tomato, chopped
8 fresh basil leaves, minced
Dijon Vinaigrette (below)
Garlic salt and pepper to taste

Boil the shrimp, bay leaf and lemon in enough water to cover in a saucepan until the shrimp turn pink; drain, discarding the bay leaf and lemon. Peel and devein the shrimp. Cook the pasta in enough water to cover in a saucepan until al dente; drain. Combine the pasta, shrimp, green onions, bell peppers, tomato and basil in a large bowl. Pour the Dijon Vinaigrette over the pasta mixture and toss well to coat. Sprinkle with garlic salt and pepper. Chill, covered, until ready to serve.

Serves 8

Dijon Vinaigrette

1/2 cup olive oil
1/4 cup vegetable oil
1 tablespoon Dijon mustard
1 teaspoon sugar
Juice of 1 lemon
Worcestershire sauce to taste

Combine the olive oil, vegetable oil, Dijon mustard, sugar, lemon juice and Worcestershire sauce in a small bowl and whisk until blended.

Makes 3/4 cup

Greek Pasta Salad

6 ounces uncooked ziti
$^1/_2$ cup plain yogurt
$^1/_2$ cup garlic salad dressing
$^1/_2$ teaspoon crushed dried oregano
$1^1/_4$ cups thinly sliced cucumber halves
$^1/_2$ cup sliced pitted black olives
1 cup crumbled feta cheese
12 cherry tomatoes, cut into quarters
1 cup alfalfa sprouts (optional)
Onion and garlic croutons

Cook the pasta in boiling water in a saucepan for 14 minutes or until tender but still slightly firm, stirring occasionally; drain. Rinse immediately with cold water; drain. Place the pasta in a large bowl. Combine the yogurt, salad dressing and oregano in a small bowl and mix well. Stir $^1/_3$ cup of the yogurt mixture into the pasta. Place in a 2-quart bowl. Layer the cucumber, olives and cheese over the pasta. Spread the remaining yogurt mixture over the top. Cover with the tomatoes and alfalfa sprouts. Chill, tightly covered, for up to 24 hours. Sprinkle with croutons just before serving.

Serves 4 to 6

Apple Salad

1 large Red Delicious apple
1 large Granny Smith apple
1 rib celery, finely chopped
$1/2$ teaspoon lemon juice
$1/4$ cup coarsely chopped pecans
$1/3$ cup raisins
$1/4$ cup mayonnaise

Rinse and dry the apples. Core the apples and cut into bite-size pieces. Combine the apples and celery in a medium bowl. Add the lemon juice and toss to coat. Stir in the pecans, raisins and mayonnaise. Chill, covered, until ready to serve.

Serves 4

Strawberry Pretzel Salad

2 cups crushed pretzels
$3/4$ cup ($1^{1}/2$ sticks) butter or margarine, melted
1 tablespoon sugar
8 ounces cream cheese, softened
8 ounces whipped topping
1 cup confectioners' sugar
2 (3-ounce) packages strawberry gelatin
2 cups boiling water
2 (10-ounce) packages frozen strawberries

Mix the pretzels, butter and sugar in a bowl. Press into a 9×13-inch glass baking dish. Bake at 400 degrees for 8 minutes. Let stand until cool. Beat the cream cheese, whipped topping and confectioners' sugar in a mixing bowl until smooth. Spread over the cooled crust. Dissolve the gelatin in the boiling water in a heatproof bowl. Add the frozen strawberries and stir until broken apart. Spread over the cream cheese mixture. Chill, covered, for 3 to 12 hours before serving.

Serves 10

Train Wreck!

6 ounces cottage cheese
6 ounces whipped topping
1 (6-ounce) package orange gelatin
1 (16-ounce) can mandarin oranges, drained
1 (16-ounce) can crushed pineapple, drained
1/2 cup pecans, chopped

Combine the cottage cheese, whipped topping and orange gelatin in a bowl and mix well. Fold in the mandarin oranges, pineapple and pecans. Spoon into a serving bowl. Chill, covered, until ready to serve.

Serves 4 to 6

Variations: Try using cherry gelatin and maraschino cherries, or strawberry gelatin and sliced strawberries, as substitutes for the orange gelatin, mandarin oranges and pineapple.

Ruby Gelatin Salad

1 (3-ounce) package cherry gelatin
1 cup boiling water
1 cup orange juice
1 cup chopped peeled apple
1 cup chopped celery
1/2 cup chopped walnuts

Dissolve the gelatin in the boiling water in a heatproof bowl. Stir in the orange juice. Pour into a serving bowl. Chill, covered, until partially set. Stir in the apple, celery and walnuts. Chill, covered, until firm. Serve on a leaf of lettuce with a dollop of mayonnaise, yogurt or whipped topping if desired.

Serves 8

The Legend of Train Wreck Salad and Other Food Tales

Did you know meals can tell a story? Some of the best recipes come from dark clouds in the kitchen that turn out to have a culinary silver lining. Legend has it this salad came about when a hostess was delayed in returning home by traffic resulting from a train wreck. Since she didn't have time for her gelatin salad to set, she combined these ingredients, and the Train Wreck salad was the delicious result. The moral of this story: don't panic when things go awry in the kitchen. By using clever substitutes from your pantry, a great story, and a sense of humor, you'll score a hit and make a memory with your guests.

The moral of this story: don't panic when things go awry in the kitchen.

Roquefort Dressing

1 cup sour cream
11 ounces cottage cheese
1 cup mayonnaise
$1/4$ cup crumbled Roquefort cheese
$1/3$ cup vinegar
1 teaspoon garlic powder
$1/4$ teaspoon salt
$1/4$ teaspoon pepper

Combine the sour cream, cottage cheese, mayonnaise, Roquefort cheese, vinegar, garlic powder, salt and pepper in a medium mixing bowl. Beat for 2 minutes. Chill, covered, for 8 to 12 hours.

Makes 3 cups

Note: Serve this wonderful dressing over wedges of iceberg lettuce. Sprinkle with chopped tomatoes, bacon bits, and chopped green onions.

Homemade Spicy Mayonnaise

2 eggs
1 tablespoon dry mustard
1 teaspoon paprika
1 teaspoon red pepper

½ teaspoon black pepper
Vegetable oil
¼ cup lemon juice
1 tablespoon salt

Process the eggs, dry mustard, paprika, red pepper and black pepper in a
blender or food processor container until blended. Add vegetable oil in
a fine stream until the mixture thickens and is of the desired consistency,
processing constantly. Add the lemon juice and salt. Continue to process
until blended, adding enough vegetable oil in a fine stream to make the
mixture the desired consistency. Store in the refrigerator.

Makes about 1 cup

Mama Net's Mustard

1 cup cider vinegar
4 ounces dry mustard

3 eggs
½ cup sugar

Combine the vinegar and mustard in a bowl and mix well. Chill,
covered, in the refrigerator for 8 to 12 hours. Combine the eggs and
sugar in a saucepan and mix well. Cook over medium heat for 2 minutes
or until thickened, stirring constantly. Add to the mustard mixture and
mix well. Pour into a sterilized 1-pint jar with a tight-fitting lid. Store,
covered, in the refrigerator.

Makes 1 pint

Note: This recipe may be doubled.

Generation After Generation

The hallmark of a good recipe in the South is often the number of generations that have enjoyed it. The recipes on these pages have been enjoyed by one of our League families for many years. Some of the recipes submitted by our members were handwritten by beloved mothers, grandmothers, aunts, and friends and passed down to younger women in the family. Junior League cookbooks like ours share these tried-and-true favorites with an even larger audience.

The recipes on these pages have been enjoyed by one of our League families for many years.

Snellville and Grayson

If "everybody's somebody in Snellville," as the local saying goes, then there are a lot of celebrities in this part of South Gwinnett County. Beginning with a small store built by Thomas Snell in the late 1800s, this burgeoning town now features major shopping centers up and down its main thoroughfare, Highway 78. All these stores are catering to a large population of newcomers to the Atlanta area that have discovered the rural charm and urban convenience of Snellville and its smaller suburb, Grayson.

Proximity to Stone Mountain Park and its recreational facilities make this area a top draw with people craving the active life. A strong parks system provides lots of opportunities for riding bikes, feeding ducks, and participating in your favorite sport. Nearby is the Yellow River Game Ranch and the Vines Botanical Gardens, both ideal day excursions for families. A popular community event is Snellville Days, a festival usually held in May. The festivities celebrate the town's heritage through parades, a craft fair, and children's activities.

Entrées

French Oven Beef Stew

2 pounds lean beef, cubed
2 medium onions, cut into eighths
3 ribs celery, diagonally sliced
4 medium carrots, diagonally sliced
1 cup vegetable juice cocktail
1/3 cup quick-cooking tapioca

1 tablespoon sugar
1 tablespoon salt
1/4 teaspoon pepper
1/2 teaspoon basil
2 medium red potatoes

Combine the beef, onions, celery, carrots, vegetable juice cocktail, tapioca, sugar, salt, pepper and basil in a 2 1/2-quart baking dish. Bake, covered, at 300 degrees for 2 1/2 hours. Cut the potatoes into 1/4-inch slices. Add to the stew and stir to mix well. Bake, uncovered, for 1 hour, stirring occasionally and adding water as needed for the desired consistency.

Serves 4 to 6

Skillet Beef Stroganoff

3 pounds round steak, 1/2 inch thick
1/4 cup flour
1/2 cup (1 stick) butter or margarine
1 large onion, finely chopped
1 (10-ounce) can beef broth
1 (10-ounce) can tomato soup

4 ounces sliced fresh mushrooms
1/2 teaspoon salt
1/4 teaspoon pepper
1/2 to 3/4 cup sour cream
Hot cooked egg noodles

Cut the steak across the grain into 1/4×2-inch strips. Dredge the steak in the flour. Melt the butter in a large skillet over medium heat. Add the beef and onion. Cook until the beef is brown. Stir in the beef broth, tomato soup, mushrooms, salt and pepper. Reduce the heat to low. Simmer, covered, for 30 to 45 minutes or until the beef is tender. Stir in the sour cream. Cook until heated through. Serve over hot cooked egg noodles.

Serves 8

Slow-Cooked Pot Roast

12 small white potatoes, peeled
1 (3-pound) boneless chuck roast
1 tablespoon vegetable oil
1 cup chopped onion
1 (15-ounce) can tomato sauce
1/4 cup packed brown sugar
3 tablespoons Worcestershire sauce
2 tablespoons cider vinegar
1 teaspoon salt

Place the potatoes in a slow cooker. Brown the beef in the oil in a skillet. Place the beef over the potatoes. Drain the skillet, reserving 1 tablespoon drippings. Add the onion to the drippings in the skillet. Sauté until tender. Stir in the tomato sauce, brown sugar, Worcestershire sauce, cider vinegar and salt. Bring to a boil. Pour over the beef. Cook on High for 4 to 5 hours. Return the sauce to a skillet just before serving. Cook over medium-high heat until thickened, stirring constantly. Serve over the beef.

Serves 6 to 8

Note: You may also prepare this recipe in an oven-cooking bag in the oven. Bake for 1 to 1 1/2 hours following the cooking bag instructions.

Slow Cooking on Fast-Forward Days

You don't need a personal chef to get dinner on the table—just fill up your slow cooker with this easy dish, plug it in, and head for the door. With little effort, your slow cooker will have dinner ready when you get home.

* Choose the right size cooker for the recipe, and fill at least half full for the best results. Sizes range from 1 to 6 quarts (1-quart units have only on-off settings, not Low-High).
* To convert a recipe to a slow cooker, reduce the amount of liquid by half, unless it's soup.
* Always cook with the cover on and no peeking until it's time to stir.
* You don't need to preheat. Use the Low setting for all-day cooking; 1 hour on High equals 2 1/2 hours on Low.
* Make cleanup easy by spraying the stoneware liner with nonstick cooking spray.

Old-Fashioned Meat Loaf

1 cup dry bread crumbs
1$\frac{1}{2}$ pounds ground chuck
$\frac{1}{4}$ cup finely chopped onion
1 egg
$\frac{1}{4}$ cup ketchup
$\frac{1}{2}$ cup milk
1$\frac{1}{2}$ teaspoons salt
$\frac{1}{4}$ teaspoon pepper
$\frac{1}{2}$ cup ketchup
$\frac{1}{4}$ cup vinegar
$\frac{1}{4}$ cup packed brown sugar
2 tablespoons Worcestershire sauce

Mix the bread crumbs and ground chuck in a large bowl. Combine the onion, egg, $\frac{1}{4}$ cup ketchup, milk, salt and pepper in a bowl and mix well. Add to the ground chuck mixture and mix well. Shape into a loaf and place in a baking dish. Heat $\frac{1}{2}$ cup ketchup, vinegar, brown sugar and Worcestershire sauce in a saucepan. Do not boil. Pour over the meat loaf. Bake at 350 degrees for 1 hour or until cooked through.

Serves 6

Note: Uncooked rolled oats may be substituted for the bread crumbs, or use $\frac{1}{2}$ of each, depending on what you have on hand.

Garden Beef and Rice

1 pound ground beef
1/2 cup chopped onion
1 garlic clove, minced
Oregano, salt and pepper
   to taste
1 (14-ounce) can chopped
   tomatoes

1 1/2 cups frozen lima beans
1 cup frozen corn
1 cup water
1 1/2 cups cooked rice
1 cup shredded Cheddar cheese

Brown the ground beef with onion and garlic in a large skillet, stirring until the ground beef is crumbly; drain. Season with oregano, salt and pepper. Stir in the tomatoes, lima beans, corn and water. Bring to a boil. Cook for 8 minutes or until the lima beans are tender. Add the rice. Cook until heated through. Remove from the heat. Sprinkle with the cheese. Cover and let stand for 3 minutes or until the cheese melts.

Serves 6

Rosemary-Crusted Roasted Lamb

2 medium garlic cloves
1 (1- to 3 1/2-pound) bone-in
   lamb shoulder roast

1/2 teaspoon rosemary
Salt and pepper to taste

Peel the garlic and cut into slivers. Make several slits in the roast. Insert the garlic in the slits. Sprinkle with rosemary. Season the outside of the roast liberally with salt and pepper. Place in a baking pan. Bake at 450 degrees for 10 minutes. Reduce the oven temperature to 350 degrees. Bake for 1 hour and 20 minutes longer or 26 minutes per pound for medium-rare. Remove from the oven. Let rest for 20 minutes to allow the juices to settle. To serve, carve the roast across the grain into 1/4-inch slices.

Serves 10

Grilled Caribbean Pork

2 (1½- to 2-pound) pork tenderloins
1 tablespoon grated fresh gingerroot
3 garlic cloves, mashed
1 tablespoon hoisin sauce
1 tablespoon black bean chili paste
2 tablespoons dark soy sauce

1 tablespoon molasses
½ teaspoon white pepper
½ cup olive oil
½ bunch cilantro, chopped
Mango Salsa (page 125)

Place the pork in a sealable food storage bag. Combine the gingerroot, garlic, hoisin sauce, chili paste, soy sauce, molasses, white pepper, olive oil and cilantro in a bowl and mix well. Pour over the pork and seal the bag. Marinate in the refrigerator for 8 to 12 hours. Drain the pork, discarding the marinade. Place the pork on a grill rack. Grill, covered, 6 inches from 300- to 400-degree coals for 12 to 14 minutes or until cooked through, turning once. Serve sliced with Mango Salsa.

Serves 12

Smoked Sesame Tenderloin

1 pound pork tenderloin
½ cup soy sauce
2 garlic cloves, minced
1 teaspoon ginger

1 tablespoon vegetable oil
¼ cup honey
3 tablespoons brown sugar
¼ cup sesame seeds

Place the tenderloin in a sealable food storage bag. Mix the soy sauce, garlic, ginger and oil in a bowl. Pour over the tenderloin and seal the bag. Marinate in the refrigerator for 2 hours. Mix the honey and brown sugar in a shallow dish. Drain the tenderloin, discarding the marinade. Roll the tenderloin in the honey mixture until well coated. Roll in the sesame seeds. Place the tenderloin on a V-rack with a drip pan. Smoke at 300 degrees for 40 minutes or until a meat thermometer inserted into the thickest portion registers 160 degrees.

Serves 6

Pulled Pork Barbecue

1 (5-pound) bone-in pork loin roast
1 medium onion, sliced, separated into rings
1 or 2 garlic cloves, sliced
3 or 4 whole garlic cloves
2 cups Barbecue Sauce (below)
1 teaspoon lemon juice
2 tablespoons red wine vinegar
Tabasco sauce to taste

Place the pork in a slow cooker. Top with the onion, sliced garlic and whole garlic cloves. Do not add any liquid. Cook on High for 5 hours or until the pork pulls apart easily. Remove to a platter to cool. Pull the pork apart and place in a large skillet or Dutch oven. Add the Barbecue Sauce, lemon juice, red wine vinegar and Tabasco sauce. Cook over medium heat until bubbly.

Serves 4 to 6

Barbecue Sauce

1/4 cup packed brown sugar
1/4 cup vinegar
1/4 cup Worcestershire sauce
1 cup ketchup
2 cups water
1 teaspoon dry mustard
1 teaspoon chili powder
Tabasco sauce to taste
Salt to taste

Combine the brown sugar, vinegar, Worcestershire sauce, ketchup, water, dry mustard, chili powder, Tabasco sauce and salt in a saucepan. Bring to a boil over medium heat. Remove from the heat. Use as a sauce or as a baste for meat.

Makes 2 1/2 cups

Which 'Cue is You?

Wars haven't been fought over the colors of barbecue sauce, but some strong words have been exchanged! "Barbecue" is a noun describing what you're eating, not how you're preparing the meat. In the South, types of barbecue and their sauces are as indicative of a state as its flag or flower. If you grew up in Georgia, you can't imagine anything other than a thick, red, ketchup-based sauce laced with brown sugar. Texans fire up their sauce with jalapeño chiles and a tomato base until it's hot, hot, hot. The Carolinas have the widest variety in color, ranging from a clear, thin vinegar-based sauce in the north to a yellow mustard and vinegar mix in the south. And if you hail from the Bluegrass State of Kentucky, you've got to have molasses and bourbon to flavor your favorite sauce and give it a deep brown color.

Pork Chops in Mushroom Sauce

6 pork chops, 1 inch thick
3 tablespoons vegetable oil
2 cups beef bouillon
1 cup fresh mushrooms, sliced
1 tablespoon minced parsley
1^1/2 teaspoons paprika
Salt and pepper to taste
1 medium onion, sliced, separated into rings
2 tablespoons cornstarch
^{3}/4 to 1 cup sour cream
Garnish: Minced parsley

Brown the pork chops in the oil in a skillet over medium-high heat. Place in an oblong baking dish. Mix the bouillon, mushrooms, 1 tablespoon parsley, paprika, salt and pepper in a medium bowl. Pour over the pork chops. Bake, covered, at 350 degrees for 45 minutes. Arrange the onion rings on top of each pork chop. Bake, covered, for 30 minutes. Remove from the oven and place the pork chops in a warm serving dish.

Pour the pan drippings into a large saucepan. Add the cornstarch. Cook over medium heat until thickened, stirring constantly. Remove from the heat. Stir in the sour cream. Pour over the top of the pork chops. Garnish with minced parsley. Serve immediately.

Serves 6

Island Barbecued Spareribs

3 pounds spareribs or Texas-style ribs
$^1/_4$ cup sugar
1 teaspoon salt
$^1/_2$ cup soy sauce
$^1/_2$ cup ketchup
3 tablespoons brown sugar
1 egg-size gingerroot, grated
1 teaspoon MSG (optional)

Place the ribs in enough water to cover in a saucepan. Bring to a boil and reduce the heat. Simmer for 15 minutes; drain. Mix the sugar and salt together. Rub on all sides of the ribs. Place in a container and cover. Chill in the refrigerator for 8 to 12 hours. Combine the soy sauce, ketchup, brown sugar, gingerroot and MSG in a bowl and mix well. Chill, covered, in the refrigerator for 8 to 12 hours.

Brush the ribs with some of the sauce and place in a baking pan. Let stand for 1 hour. Bake, covered with foil, at 325 degrees for $1^1/_2$ hours. Remove the foil. Bake for 30 minutes longer, basting with the remaining sauce every 15 minutes.

Serves 6

From the Wine List

Pork entrées are a common sight on southern dinner tables, with variations ranging from down-home favorites to island-spiced exotics. Traditional wine pairings with pork start with gewürztraminer, a white wine with a spicy-sweet flavor. Its grapes are commonly found in Germany ("gewürz" is German for "spiced"), California, and Alsace, France. For something completely different, try Châteauneuf-du-Pape (Shah-toe-nuff-dew-POP), a full-bodied red wine from France that has exotic tastes of cocoa and red berries. You'll know it by the distinctive embossing on the bottle.

Traditional wine pairings with pork start with gewürztraminer...

Pizza Bread

3 eggs
1 tablespoon oregano
3 tablespoons grated Parmesan
  cheese

2 loaves frozen bread dough, thawed
11 ounces pepperoni, sliced
1 round provolone cheese, shredded

Beat the eggs, oregano and Parmesan cheese in a mixing bowl. Roll the bread dough into two 8×14-inch rectangles. Reserve 3 tablespoons of the egg mixture. Spread the remaining egg mixture over the rectangles. Layer the pepperoni and provolone cheese over the egg mixture. Roll up each rectangle as for a jelly roll and seal the ends. Place seam side down in a baking pan. Brush with the reserved egg mixture. Bake at 350 degrees for 35 to 40 minutes or until golden brown.

Makes 2 loaves

Creamy Chicken Enchiladas

1 tablespoon butter or margarine
1 medium onion, chopped
1 (4-ounce) can chopped green
  chiles, drained
8 ounces cream cheese, chopped,
  softened

$3^{1}/_{2}$ cups chopped cooked chicken
  breasts
8 (8-inch) flour tortillas
16 ounces Monterey Jack cheese,
  shredded
2 cups heavy cream

Melt the butter in a large skillet over medium heat. Add the onion. Sauté for 5 minutes. Add the green chiles. Sauté for 1 minute. Stir in the cream cheese and chicken. Cook until the cream cheese melts, stirring constantly. Spoon 2 to 3 tablespoons chicken mixture down the center of each tortilla. Roll up and place seam side down in a lightly greased 9×13-inch baking dish. Sprinkle with Monterey Jack cheese. Drizzle with the heavy cream. Bake at 350 degrees for 45 minutes.

Serves 4 or 5

Note: To lighten this rich sauce, use picante sauce instead of the heavy cream.

Chicken Packets

2 tablespoons olive oil
4 boneless skinless chicken breasts, cut into 1-inch pieces
1 cup chopped onion
1/2 cup chopped green bell pepper or celery
1/2 cup sour cream
2/3 cup cream of mushroom soup
1/2 teaspoon garlic salt
1/4 teaspoon pepper
3 (8-ounce) cans crescent rolls
1 cup shredded mozzarella cheese

Heat the olive oil in a medium skillet over medium-high heat. Add the chicken, onion and bell pepper. Sauté for 5 minutes or until the chicken is tender and cooked through; drain. Combine the chicken mixture, sour cream, mushroom soup, garlic salt and pepper in a bowl and mix well. Unroll the crescent roll dough. Separate into 12 rectangles and press the perforations to seal. Spoon 2 tablespoons of the chicken mixture in the center of each rectangle. Sprinkle evenly with mozzarella cheese. Bring the corners of the rectangles together and twist, pinching the seams to seal. Place on a lightly greased baking sheet. Bake at 350 degrees for 20 minutes or until golden brown.

Serves 6

Note: Make this quick and easy weeknight meal by using chicken that has been cooked ahead. Your family will love it.

A Night Under the Stars

Belly dancers, a camel in the hallway, and Arabian lanterns—does this sound like a typical Junior League event? It does if you're talking about the STAR Ball, our annual formal ball and silent auction. Ball attendees have the opportunity to bid on a wide variety of items graciously donated by area merchants, making this our major fund-raiser.

The black-tie gala was named for STAR House, an after-school program for at-risk children started by our League in 1993. Since its successful inception, the event has grown in scope to benefit all the projects the JLGNF supports. Some of these have included the Norcross Cooperative Ministries, North Fulton Community Charities, and Big Brothers and Big Sisters.

Chicken Breasts Stuffed with Cheese

4 boneless skinless chicken breasts,
   cut into halves
Salt and pepper to taste
1/2 cup (1 stick) butter, softened
2 tablespoons parsley
1 teaspoon marjoram
1/2 teaspoon thyme

4 ounces mozzarella cheese
1/2 cup flour
2 eggs, beaten
1 cup bread crumbs
Paprika to taste
1/2 to 1 cup white wine

Pound the chicken thin. Sprinkle with salt and pepper. Spread 1/2 of the butter over the chicken. Melt the remaining butter with the parsley, marjoram and thyme in a saucepan. Cut the mozzarella cheese into 8 sticks. Place in the center of the chicken. Roll up, tucking in the ends to seal. Roll in the flour. Dip in the eggs and roll in the bread crumbs. Place in a baking dish sprayed with nonstick cooking spray. Drizzle the herb butter over the chicken. Sprinkle with paprika. Bake at 350 degrees for 20 minutes. Pour the wine evenly over the chicken. Bake for 15 to 20 minutes or until the chicken is cooked through, basting frequently with the pan juices.

Serves 4

Chicken Monte Carlo

4 boneless skinless chicken breasts
1 (10-ounce) package frozen
   chopped broccoli
1 (10-ounce) can cream of
   chicken soup
1/2 cup mayonnaise

Dash of lemon juice
8 ounces Cheddar cheese, shredded
8 ounces stuffing mix
2 tablespoons butter, melted
Paprika to taste
Slivered almonds (optional)

Boil the chicken in water to cover in a saucepan until cooked through; drain. Cut into bite-size pieces. Cook the broccoli using the package directions; drain. Mix the chicken soup, mayonnaise and lemon juice in a small bowl. Place the broccoli in a 2 1/2-quart shallow baking dish. Layer the chicken, soup mixture, Cheddar cheese and stuffing mix over the broccoli. Drizzle with the melted butter. Sprinkle with paprika and almonds. Bake at 350 degrees for 30 minutes.

Serves 4

Swiss Chicken Bake

8 boneless skinless chicken
   breasts
8 (4×4-inch) slices Swiss cheese
1 (10-ounce) can cream of
   chicken soup or cream of
   mushroom soup
$^1/_4$ cup dry white wine
$1^1/_2$ teaspoons rosemary
$1^1/_2$ teaspoons tarragon
$^1/_4$ cup milk
1 cup herb stuffing mix
3 tablespoons butter, melted

Place the chicken in an 8×12-inch baking dish lightly sprayed with
nonstick cooking spray. Arrange the Swiss cheese over the chicken.
Combine the soup, wine, rosemary, tarragon and milk in a bowl and mix
well. Spoon over the chicken. Sprinkle with the stuffing mix. Drizzle
with the butter. Cover with foil. Bake at 350 degrees for 45 minutes.
Serve with hot cooked rice and a favorite vegetable.

Serves 8

Crusty Parmesan Chicken

2 cups dry bread crumbs
$^3/_4$ cup grated Parmesan cheese
$^1/_4$ cup chopped fresh parsley
$1^1/_2$ teaspoons paprika
$1^1/_2$ teaspoons garlic salt
$1^1/_2$ teaspoons pepper
$^3/_4$ cup ($1^1/_2$ sticks) unsalted
   butter
1 teaspoon Worcestershire sauce
1 teaspoon dry mustard
12 boneless skinless chicken
   breasts

Line a 9×13-inch baking dish with foil. Mix the bread crumbs, Parmesan
cheese, parsley, paprika, garlic salt and pepper in a bowl. Melt the butter
in a saucepan. Stir in the Worcestershire sauce and dry mustard. Dip the
chicken in the butter mixture. Roll in the crumb mixture until coated.
Arrange in the prepared baking dish. Pour the remaining butter mixture
over the chicken. Bake at 350 degrees for 50 to 60 minutes or until the
chicken is cooked through.

Serves 12

*Note: This recipe may also be prepared as an appetizer by cutting the chicken into strips
and baking for about 30 minutes. Serve with honey mustard sauce for dipping. Makes
about 36 appetizers.*

Hot Chicken Salad

4 cups chopped cooked chicken
2 cups chopped celery
1 cup mayonnaise
1/2 cup sliced almonds, toasted
1/2 cup sliced water chestnuts
1 (10-ounce) can cream of celery
  soup or mushroom soup
1 soup can water
2 tablespoons lemon juice
1 teaspoon grated onion
1 cup crushed potato chips
1 cup shredded sharp Cheddar
  cheese

Combine the chicken, celery, mayonnaise, almonds and water chestnuts in a large bowl and mix well. Add the soup, water, lemon juice and onion and mix well. Spoon into a 9×13-inch baking dish. Sprinkle with the potato chips. Bake at 350 degrees for 20 to 30 minutes or until bubbly. Sprinkle with the cheese. Bake until the cheese melts.

Serves 6

Variation: Omit the sliced almonds from the chicken filling. Unroll an 8-ounce can of crescent roll dough and press the perforations to seal. Use instead of the potato chips to cover the top. Sprinkle the top with a mixture of the cheese and sliced almonds during the last 5 minutes of baking.

Skillet Chicken Parmigiana

1 egg, beaten
1/2 cup Italian bread crumbs
4 boneless skinless chicken breasts
1/4 cup vegetable oil
1 (26-ounce) jar spaghetti sauce
1 1/2 cups water
8 ounces uncooked spaghetti, broken
1/2 cup shredded mozzarella cheese

Place the egg and bread crumbs in separate shallow dishes. Dip the chicken into the egg and roll in the bread crumbs to coat. Heat the oil in a large deep skillet over medium-high heat. Add the chicken. Sauté for 5 to 6 minutes on each side or until the chicken is cooked through. Remove the chicken to a platter to keep warm, reserving the drippings in the skillet. Add the spaghetti sauce, water and spaghetti to the skillet. Cook for 5 to 7 minutes or until the spaghetti is tender. Reduce the heat to medium-low. Place the chicken over the spaghetti in the skillet. Sprinkle with the cheese. Cook, covered, for 4 to 5 minutes or until the cheese melts and the chicken is heated through.

Serves 4

Grilled Thanksgiving Turkey

1 (12- to 16-pound) frozen Carolina tom turkey
Granulated garlic, black pepper and cayenne pepper to taste
2 (15-ounce) cans chunk pineapple, drained
2 large garlic cloves, chopped
2 cups honey
1 cup Kahlúa (coffee liqueur)

Thaw the turkey using the package directions. Discard the bag in the cavity. Rub the turkey with granulated garlic, black pepper and cayenne pepper. Place the pineapple and chopped garlic in the turkey cavity. Heat the honey in a saucepan over low heat. Add the Kahlúa gradually, stirring constantly.

Prepare the grill using a 20-pound bag of charcoal and cherry, mesquite or pecan wood. Place the turkey on the grill rack. Grill over hot coals for 1 hour. Baste with the Kahlúa sauce. Grill, covered, for 3 hours. Uncover and baste with the Kahlúa sauce. Grill, covered, for 3 hours longer. Wrap the turkey in foil. Place in a 150-degree oven until ready to serve.

Serves 24 to 32

Note: You may bake the turkey in a 250-degree oven, basting with the Kahlúa sauce in 3 hour-increments as above. This method is more convenient, but the flavor of the charcoal and wood will be lost.

From the Wine List

Once a year, on the third Thursday in November, wine aficionados everywhere line up at their restaurants and retailers. Why? That's the annual release date of Beaujolais Nouveau, a soft and fruity wine made in the Beaujolais region of France. What makes this wine unique is that the grape is picked, fermented, bottled, and shipped within the space of a few weeks, rather than months or years. Because of its release date, Beaujolais Nouveau has earned the nickname "Thanksgiving Wine" in the United States. But don't hold onto your prize past New Year's Day. Beaujolais Nouveau is meant to be enjoyed within six months of bottling.

Because of its release date, Beaujolais Nouveau has earned the nickname "Thanksgiving Wine" in the United States.

97

Chicken Tetrazzini

1 medium onion, chopped
3/4 cup chopped green bell pepper
1 cup chopped celery
1/2 cup (1 stick) margarine
1 tablespoon flour
1 cup shredded Cheddar cheese
1 (10-ounce) can cream of
   mushroom soup
2 (15-ounce) cans chicken broth

1 teaspoon salt
1/2 teaspoon celery salt
2 1/2 cups chopped cooked chicken
1/2 cup sliced mushrooms
1/2 cup slivered almonds
1 (2-ounce) jar chopped pimentos,
   drained
1 pound spaghetti, cooked, drained
1 cup cracker crumbs (optional)

Sauté the onion, bell pepper and celery in the margarine in a skillet until tender. Add the flour, cheese and soup and stir to blend well. Add the broth, stirring until smooth. Add the salt, celery salt, chicken, mushrooms, almonds and pimentos and mix well. Add the spaghetti and toss to mix well. Spoon into a large baking dish. Sprinkle with the cracker crumbs. Bake at 400 degrees for 20 minutes.

Serves 8

Gourmet Grouper Fillets

3/4 cup grated Parmesan cheese
1/2 cup (1 stick) butter, softened
3 tablespoons mayonnaise
3 tablespoons chopped green onions
2 teaspoons chopped chives

6 (8-ounce) grouper or other mild
   white fish fillets, 1 inch thick
1/4 cup lemon juice
Pepper to taste
Garnish: Lemon slices and chives

Combine the Parmesan cheese, butter, mayonnaise, green onions and 2 teaspoons chives in a small bowl and mix well. Place the fish on a lightly greased rack in a broiler pan. Drizzle with the lemon juice and sprinkle with pepper. Broil 6 inches from the heat source for 8 to 10 minutes or until the fish flakes easily. Remove from the oven. Spread the fish with the Parmesan cheese mixture. Return to the oven. Broil for 2 minutes or until the Parmesan cheese mixture is light brown and bubbly. Garnish with lemon slices and chives.

Serves 6

Shrimp and Chicken Bake

1 (8-ounce) package yellow rice
1 cup (2 sticks) butter
$^{1}/_{2}$ cup flour
3 pounds boneless skinless chicken breasts,
   cooked, chopped
3 pounds shrimp, cooked, peeled
4 cups half-and-half
1 cup shredded longhorn or Cheddar cheese
$^{1}/_{4}$ teaspoon red pepper
1 cup sliced mushrooms
$^{1}/_{2}$ cup chopped artichoke hearts

Prepare the rice using the package directions. Melt the butter in a Dutch oven over medium heat. Add the flour. Cook until smooth, whisking constantly. Add the chicken, shrimp, half-and-half, cheese, red pepper, mushrooms and artichokes. Cook until bubbly, stirring constantly. Remove from the heat.

Divide the rice between 2 buttered 9×13-inch glass baking dishes. Pour the chicken and shrimp mixture over the rice. Bake at 350 degrees for 30 minutes.

Serves 12 to 16

Note: This is a great recipe for a buffet.

Shrimp and Grits Casserole

5 cups water
1$\frac{1}{2}$ pounds unpeeled medium fresh shrimp
3$\frac{1}{4}$ cups water
$\frac{1}{2}$ teaspoon salt
1 cup uncooked regular grits
2 eggs, lightly beaten
$\frac{1}{4}$ cup milk
2 garlic cloves, minced
1$\frac{1}{2}$ cups shredded Cheddar cheese
Garnish: Chopped fresh parsley

Bring 5 cups water to a boil in a stockpot. Add the shrimp. Cook for 3 to
5 minutes or until the shrimp turn pink. Drain well and rinse with cold water.
Peel and devein the shrimp.

Bring 3$\frac{1}{4}$ cups water and salt to a boil in a medium saucepan. Stir in the grits.
Cover and reduce the heat. Simmer for 10 minutes. Remove from the heat.
Combine the eggs and milk in a large bowl and beat well. Add the grits gradually,
stirring constantly. Stir in the shrimp, garlic and 1 cup of the cheese.

Spoon into a lightly greased 7×11-inch baking dish. Sprinkle with the remaining
$\frac{1}{2}$ cup cheese. Bake at 350 degrees for 30 minutes. Let stand for 5 minutes.
Garnish with parsley.

Serves 6

Corn Bread Shrimp Supreme

3 thick slices bacon
4 eggs
1/4 cup milk
1/2 cup (1 stick) butter, melted, cooled
1 (6-ounce) package corn bread mix
6 dashes of hot sauce
1 medium onion, chopped
1 (10-ounce) package frozen chopped broccoli or spinach,
    thawed, drained
1 pound shrimp, cooked, peeled, deveined, coarsely chopped
2 cups shredded Cheddar cheese
Garnish: Chopped fresh parsley

Cook the bacon in a 10-inch cast-iron skillet until crisp. Remove the
bacon to paper towels to drain. Crumble the bacon. Drain the skillet,
reserving 1 tablespoon bacon drippings. Wipe the skillet clean with a
paper towel. Return the reserved bacon drippings to the skillet. Place
the skillet in a 375-degree oven.

Beat the eggs in a large bowl. Add the milk, butter, corn bread mix and
hot sauce and mix well. Stir in the onion, broccoli, shrimp and 1 1/2 cups
of the cheese. Pour into the hot skillet. Sprinkle with the remaining
1/2 cup cheese. Bake at 375 degrees for 30 to 35 minutes or until golden
brown. Sprinkle with the crumbled bacon. Garnish with chopped
fresh parsley.

Serves 8

*Variation: You may use 1 pound of ground sausage, browned and drained, instead of
the shrimp.*

Shrimp, Simplified

*It wouldn't be a beach
vacation without at least one
meal of boiled shrimp. The
difference between jumbo,
large, and medium shrimp is
merely the count or number
of shrimp it takes to equal
1 pound. Approximately
2 pounds of raw, headless
shrimp yields 1 pound of
cooked, peeled, deveined
shrimp. You need to use
roughly 3/4 pound of
unpeeled shrimp per person
when preparing an entrée.*

*The secret to keeping boiled
shrimp from getting tough
is to add salt to the shrimp
after it has boiled. To devein,
use kitchen shears to make
a cut up the back of the
shrimp, leaving the tail
intact, then pull out the vein
and remove the shell.*

The secret to keeping
boiled shrimp from
getting tough is to
add salt to the shrimp
after it has boiled.

Country Ham and Shrimp on Grits

½ cup (1 stick) butter
12 ounces country ham, chopped
3 garlic cloves, finely chopped
1 green onion, chopped
½ cup brandy
2 cups heavy cream
¼ teaspoon cayenne pepper

⅓ teaspoon sage
1½ pounds small shrimp, peeled, deveined
3 tablespoons Italian parsley, chopped
Hot cooked grits

Melt the butter in a large heavy nonstick skillet over high heat. Add the ham and sauté quickly. Add the garlic and green onion. Sauté for 1 minute. Remove from the heat. Stir in the brandy. Return to the heat. Stir in the cream, cayenne pepper and sage. Cook for 3 minutes or until thickened, stirring constantly. Add the shrimp. Simmer for 2 minutes or until the shrimp turn light pink. Stir in the parsley. Serve over hot cooked grits.

Serves 4

Lowcountry Shrimp Boil

2 to 3 ribs celery
Old Bay or Zatarain's seafood seasoning packet
Salt to taste
4 ounces smoked link sausage per person, cut into 2-inch pieces

2 new potatoes per person
1½ to 2 small ears of corn per person
8 ounces unpeeled shrimp per person
Dash of Tabasco sauce

Fill a large stockpot with enough water to cover all of the ingredients. Bring to a boil. Add the celery, seafood seasoning packet and salt. Add the sausage and potatoes. Boil for 7 minutes. Add the corn on the cob. Boil for 7 minutes. Add the shrimp and Tabasco sauce. Cook for 4 minutes or until the shrimp turn pink. Do not overcook. Drain, discarding the celery and seafood seasoning packet. Serve in a large bowl or tub for a casual meal with salad and French bread. Or, if weather permits, serve outside on a table lined with newspaper for easy cleanup.

Makes a variable amount

Shrimp Scampi

8 ounces uncooked thin spaghetti
1/2 cup (1 stick) butter
1 or 2 garlic cloves, minced
1 pound uncooked shrimp, peeled, deveined
1/2 cup sliced mushrooms
Shredded Romano or Parmesan cheese to taste
Salt and pepper to taste

Cook the spaghetti using the package directions; drain. Melt the butter in a large skillet over medium heat. Add the garlic, shrimp and mushrooms. Sauté for 5 minutes or until the shrimp turn pink. Add the cooked spaghetti, Romano cheese, salt and pepper and stir carefully with a large spoon until combined.

Serves 2

Tomato Pie

1 baked (10-inch) deep-dish pie shell
3 ripe tomatoes, thickly sliced
Salt and pepper to taste
1 teaspoon basil
1 tablespoon chopped chives
1 cup mayonnaise
1 cup shredded Cheddar cheese

Fill the cooled pie shell with the tomato slices. Sprinkle with salt, pepper, basil and chives. Mix the mayonnaise and cheese in a bowl. Spread over the tomatoes. Bake at 350 degrees for 30 minutes.

Serves 4 to 6

Make It a Movie Night!

Is football season over? Whew! Now you can use that new big-screen TV as the centerpiece of your next grown-up dinner party. Everyone can appreciate a good James Bond flick, so pick your favorite and make up a premiere pitcher of martinis (shaken, not stirred, of course). Turn your coffee table into a buffet filled with cheese and crackers, an easy Caesar salad and Shrimp Scampi (at left). Relax with White Chocolate Cheesecake (from our Desserts chapter on page 129) and coffee. You choose the movie and let your guests bring a potluck menu based on the theme. The possibilities are endless.

Now you can use that new big-screen TV as the centerpiece of your next grown-up dinner party.

Vegetable Lasagna

2 eggs
2 cups reduced-fat cream-style
  cottage cheese
15 ounces reduced-fat ricotta cheese
1½ teaspoons crushed Italian
  seasoning
2 tablespoons butter or margarine
2 cups sliced fresh mushrooms
1 small onion, chopped
1 garlic clove, minced
2 tablespoons flour
½ to 1 teaspoon pepper
1¼ cups skim milk

2 (10-ounce) packages frozen
  chopped spinach or broccoli,
  thawed, drained
1 medium carrot, shredded
¾ cup shredded Parmesan cheese
Salt to taste
9 oven-ready lasagna noodles
2 cups shredded part-skim mozzarella
  cheese
1 cup shredded sharp Cheddar
  cheese
¾ cup marinara sauce

Beat the eggs lightly in a medium bowl. Stir in the cottage cheese, ricotta cheese and Italian seasoning. Melt the butter in a skillet over medium heat. Add the mushrooms, onion and garlic. Sauté until tender. Stir in the flour and pepper. Add the milk. Cook until thickened and bubbly, stirring constantly. Cook for 1 minute longer. Remove from the heat. Stir in the spinach, carrot, ½ cup of the Parmesan cheese and salt.

Layer ⅓ of the spinach mixture and ⅓ of the noodles in a greased 9×13-inch baking dish. Layer the cottage cheese mixture, the remaining spinach mixture, mozzarella cheese, Cheddar cheese and remaining noodles ½ at a time over the layers. Spread the marinara sauce over the top. Sprinkle with the remaining ¼ cup Parmesan cheese. Bake, uncovered, at 350 degrees for 35 minutes or until heated through. Let stand for 10 minutes before serving.

Serves 10 to 12

Note: You may assemble the lasagna, cover with foil and chill for up to 48 hours before baking. To freeze, wrap the unbaked lasagna tightly with foil. Freeze for up to 2 months. To serve, bake, covered, at 350 degrees for 45 minutes. Uncover and bake for 35 to 40 minutes longer or until hot and bubbly. Let stand for 15 minutes before serving.

Marinade for Beef

$2/3$ cup soy sauce
$2/3$ cup Worcestershire sauce
$1/3$ cup Jack Daniel's
Brown sugar to taste

Combine the soy sauce, Worcestershire sauce, whiskey and brown sugar in a bowl and mix well. Use to marinate beef in the refrigerator for several hours, turning occasionally.

Makes enough for 4 to 5 pounds of beef

Sweet-and-Sour Marinade

1 cup Italian salad dressing
$1/4$ cup Jack Daniel's
3 tablespoons pineapple preserves, or to taste
1 tablespoon honey
1 tablespoon soy sauce
1 teaspoon chopped garlic in oil

Combine the salad dressing, whiskey, preserves, honey, soy sauce and garlic in a bowl and mix well. Use to marinate pork or chicken in the refrigerator for 8 to 12 hours, turning every 3 hours.

Makes enough for 4 to 5 pounds of pork or chicken

Buford

With a historic town square and the new Mall of Georgia within its town limits, Buford is a prime example of how well the old and new can meld. Newcomers to this northern Gwinnett town can enjoy modern conveniences and still show off turn-of-the-century homes to their visitors. Careful attention to old and new has made Buford a town that looks ahead without neglecting its past.

When Bona Allen opened a tannery in Buford in 1873, he started a business that brought prosperity to Buford, even through the Depression. The Bona Allen mansion in downtown Buford is listed on the National Register of Historic Places. Cottages and homes built by employees line the railroad tracks that run through the center of town. These homes are being bought and renovated by families eager to preserve a strong sense of history. The arts community has embraced Buford. The Buford Artist Colony has lined Main Street in downtown with galleries and studios.

Side Dishes

Chuckwagon Beans

1 pound ground beef
1/2 cup chopped onion
1/2 cup chopped green bell pepper
3 (16-ounce) cans pork and beans

1 cup ketchup
1/2 cup packed brown sugar
1 tablespoon prepared mustard
1 tablespoon Worcestershire sauce

Brown the ground beef with the onion and bell pepper in a large skillet over medium heat, stirring until the ground beef is crumbly; drain. Add the pork and beans, ketchup, brown sugar, mustard and Worcestershire sauce and mix well. Pour into a 9×13-inch glass baking dish sprayed lightly with nonstick cooking spray. Bake, covered, at 350 degrees for 45 minutes.

Serves 12

Five-Bean Bake

8 to 10 slices bacon
2 large onions, sliced
1 cup packed brown sugar
1/2 teaspoon garlic powder
1 teaspoon salt
1/2 cup vinegar
2 (16-ounce) cans butter beans, drained

1 (16-ounce) can green beans, drained
1 (16-ounce) can lima beans, drained
1 (16-ounce) can red kidney beans, drained
1 (16-ounce) can Boston baked beans

Cook the bacon in a large skillet over medium heat until crisp. Remove the bacon to paper towels to drain. Drain the skillet, leaving enough bacon drippings to cover the bottom of the skillet. Add the onions. Sauté for 5 minutes or until transparent. Add the brown sugar, garlic powder, salt and vinegar. Simmer for 20 minutes, stirring frequently. Combine the butter beans, green beans, lima beans, red kidney beans and Boston baked beans in a large bowl and mix well. Pour into a 9×13-inch baking dish. Layer the onion mixture over the beans. Crumble the bacon over the top. Bake at 350 degrees for 1 hour.

Serves 10 to 12

Note: This recipe is good served hot or cold.

Broccoli Rice Casserole

2 (10-ounce) packages frozen broccoli
3/4 cup chopped onion
1 cup uncooked rice, cooked
1 (10-ounce) can cream of mushroom soup
1 egg, beaten
1 cup mayonnaise
1 cup shredded sharp Cheddar cheese
Salt and pepper to taste
1 cup butter cracker crumbs
1/4 cup (1/2 stick) butter, melted

Cook the broccoli using the package directions; drain. Chop the broccoli and place in a large bowl. Add the onion, rice, soup, egg, mayonnaise, cheese, salt and pepper and mix well. Pour into a 2 1/2-quart baking dish. Sprinkle with the cracker crumbs. Drizzle with the melted butter. Bake at 350 degrees for 40 minutes.

Serves 6 to 8

Glazed Carrots

1 pound baby carrots
3 tablespoons butter
1 tablespoon brown sugar
1 tablespoon orange juice

Place the carrots in a medium saucepan and cover with water. Bring to a boil. Cook for 15 minutes or until tender; drain. Add the butter, brown sugar and orange juice. Cover and let stand for 5 minutes or until the butter melts. Toss to coat evenly and serve.

Serves 6

Corn Casserole

¹/₂ cup (1 stick) butter or margarine
2 eggs
1 cup sour cream
1 (15-ounce) can cream-style corn
1 (15-ounce) can whole kernel corn
1 (6-ounce) package corn bread mix

Melt the butter in a 2-quart baking dish. Beat the eggs and sour cream in a medium mixing bowl with a whisk or fork. Stir in the cream-style corn, whole kernel corn and corn bread mix. Pour into the prepared dish. Bake at 350 degrees for 1 hour.

Serves 6

Roasted Corn

4 medium ears of fresh corn
¹/₄ cup (¹/₂ stick) butter, melted
Salt and seasoned pepper to taste

Remove the husks and silks from the corn. Place each ear of corn on a piece of heavy-duty foil. Drizzle each with 1 tablespoon butter. Season with salt and seasoned pepper. Roll the foil lengthwise around the corn and twist the foil ends to seal. Bake at 500 degrees for 20 minutes.

Serves 4

Peppered Green Beans

4 cups 1-inch snapped fresh green beans
2 tablespoons minced onion
1/2 teaspoon freshly ground pepper
1 beef bouillon cube

Place the green beans in a large saucepan and cover with water. Bring to a boil. Add the onion, pepper and bouillon cube. Reduce the heat to medium-high. Cook for 20 to 30 minutes or until the desired degree of tenderness.

Serves 6

Note: You may use two 16-ounce cans of green beans instead of the fresh green beans.

Green Bean Bundles

8 slices bacon
2 (16-ounce) cans whole green beans
6 tablespoons margarine
1/2 cup packed brown sugar
Garlic powder, salt and pepper to taste

Cut the bacon slices into halves. Wrap each half around 6 to 8 green beans and secure with a wooden pick. Place in a baking dish. Melt the margarine in a saucepan. Add the brown sugar, garlic powder, salt and pepper. Heat until the brown sugar dissolves. Pour over the green bean bundles. Bake, covered, at 375 degrees for 40 minutes. Bake, uncovered, for 5 minutes longer or until the bacon is brown.

Serves 8

How to Know Beans

Green beans (once called string beans) are stringless today—just break off the ends as you wash them. Green beans, wax beans, and pole beans may all be prepared the same way— cooked just until tender but crunchy. If left whole, the beans will be less watery and more flavorful. However, if they are thick, you may want to "French," or diagonally, slice them. The type of green beans you use doesn't make as much difference in the cooking time required as the maturity or size of the bean. Younger, more slender beans take about 8 to 10 minutes to cook; more mature beans that are thicker take about 10 to 12 minutes. When serving beans, count on 1 pound feeding 3 to 4 people.

The type of green beans you use doesn't make as much difference in the cooking time required as the maturity or size of the bean.

Green Beans with Honey Cashew Sauce

1/2 cup salted cashews, coarsely chopped
3 tablespoons unsalted butter
2 tablespoons honey
1 pound fresh green beans, blanched, drained

Sauté the cashews in the butter in a skillet over low heat for 5 minutes. Add the honey. Cook for 1 minute, stirring constantly. Pour over the green beans in a bowl and toss until coated.

Serves 4

Note: This sauce is also good served over broccoli or carrots.

Lemon Sautéed Green Beans

8 ounces fresh green beans, trimmed, snapped (about 4 cups)
Salt to taste
Olive oil
1 tablespoon lemon juice

Place the green beans in a Dutch oven and cover with water. Season with salt. Bring to a boil. Cook for 30 minutes or until the desired degree of tenderness; drain. Pour enough olive oil into a large skillet to cover the bottom. Add the lemon juice and green beans. Sauté for 10 to 15 minutes.

Serves 4

Southern Greens

1 pound lean bacon or smoked pork shoulder
3 quarts water
Freshly ground pepper to taste
Salt to taste
3 pounds turnip, collard or mustard greens, trimmed, rinsed, chopped

Place the bacon and water in a large saucepan. Season with pepper. Bring to a boil. Cover and reduce the heat. Simmer for 1 hour. Season with salt and pepper. Add the greens. Simmer, uncovered, for 15 to 17 minutes or until tender.

Serves 6

Hoppin' John

1 to 1¹/₂ cups chopped ham
1 cup finely chopped onion
¹/₂ teaspoon hot pepper sauce
2 tablespoons vegetable oil
2 (15-ounce) cans black-eyed peas, heated
3 cups cooked rice
¹/₂ teaspoon salt
Garnish: Thinly sliced ham

Sauté the chopped ham, onion and hot pepper sauce in the vegetable oil in a saucepan over medium heat for 3 to 5 minutes or until the onion is soft but not brown. Stir in the undrained black-eyed peas and rice. Cook over medium heat until heated through. Season with salt. Garnish with thinly sliced ham.

Serves 8

Happy New Year, Y'all!

The first day of a new year is yet another opportunity to celebrate with family and friends and have a feast. For years, southerners have looked to food for comfort from what lies ahead in the New Year. Every southerner hoping for prosperity will imbibe in the traditional lucky foods, like black-eyed peas for prosperity and collard greens for money. Fashion a menu from the side dishes on these pages and invite your northern neighbors over for a delicious financial investment for the New Year.

For years, southerners have looked to food for comfort from what lies ahead in the New Year.

Vidalia Onion Casserole

4 medium Vidalia onions, sliced 1/4 inch thick
1/2 cup (1 stick) margarine
12 saltines, crushed
1 (10-ounce) can cream of mushroom soup
2 eggs, beaten
1/2 to 3/4 cup milk
1 cup shredded Cheddar cheese

Sauté the onions in the margarine in a skillet until tender. Reserve 3 tablespoons of the cracker crumbs. Line a buttered 8×11-inch baking dish with the remaining cracker crumbs. Alternate layers of the sautéed onions and soup in the prepared dish until all of the ingredients are used. Cover the top with the beaten eggs. Pour the milk over the layers. Sprinkle with the cheese and reserved cracker crumbs. Bake at 350 degrees for 20 to 30 minutes or until brown and bubbly.

Serves 10 to 12

Potato, Onion and Cheddar Gratin

3 tablespoons butter
1 large onion, thinly sliced
2 pounds potatoes, peeled, thinly sliced
2 cups shredded sharp Cheddar cheese
Salt and freshly ground pepper to taste
Grated nutmeg to taste
1 1/4 cups chicken broth

Melt the butter in a skillet over medium heat. Add the onion. Sauté until tender. Alternate layers of the sautéed onion, potatoes and Cheddar cheese in a buttered 1 1/2-quart shallow baking dish, seasoning each layer with salt, pepper and nutmeg. Pour the broth over the layers. Bake, covered, at 350 degrees for 45 minutes. Bake, uncovered, for 15 to 20 minutes longer or until the top is light brown and the potatoes are tender. Serve hot.

Serves 6

Three-Cheese Mashed Potatoes

2½ pounds potatoes, peeled, cooked, mashed
½ cup (1 stick) butter, softened
6 ounces cream cheese, softened
¼ cup (or more) milk
1 cup shredded Cheddar cheese
½ cup grated Parmesan cheese
1 (2-ounce) jar pimentos, drained
3 green onions, chopped
½ cup chopped green bell pepper
Salt and pepper to taste
Garnish: Shredded Cheddar cheese

Beat the potatoes, butter, cream cheese and milk in a bowl until blended. Fold in 1 cup Cheddar cheese, Parmesan cheese, pimentos, green onions, bell pepper, salt and pepper. Spoon into a baking dish lightly sprayed with nonstick cooking spray. Bake at 350 degrees for 30 minutes or until bubbly. Garnish with Cheddar cheese. Bake for 5 minutes longer.

Serves 8

Horseradish Whipped Potatoes

6 medium white potatoes
1 teaspoon salt
¼ cup (½ stick) butter
1 cup sour cream
2 tablespoons prepared horseradish
Salt and pepper to taste

Peel the potatoes and cut into 1-inch cubes. Place in a large saucepan or Dutch oven and cover with water. Sprinkle with the salt. Bring to a boil over high heat. Reduce the heat to medium. Simmer, covered, for 20 minutes or until the potatoes are tender. Drain the potatoes and return to the saucepan. Add the butter and cover. Let stand until the butter melts. Place the potato mixture in a medium mixing bowl. Add the sour cream, horseradish and salt and pepper to taste and beat until smooth, adding additional sour cream or milk if needed for the desired consistency. Serve immediately.

Serves 6

Parmesan Potato Slices

3 baking potatoes, sliced 1/4 inch thick
1/3 cup butter, melted
Garlic salt or seasoned salt to taste
Seasoned pepper to taste
1/3 cup grated Parmesan cheese

Arrange the potatoes slightly overlapping in a single layer on a greased baking sheet. Pour the butter over the potatoes. Sprinkle with garlic salt, seasoned pepper and Parmesan cheese. Cover with foil. Bake at 350 degrees for 45 minutes. Remove the foil. Bake for 10 to 15 minutes longer or until golden brown.

Serves 6

Note: These can be baked early in the day and reheated in the oven for 20 minutes before serving.

Hash Brown Casserole

2 pounds frozen hash brown potatoes, thawed
1/2 cup (1 stick) margarine, melted
1 teaspoon salt
1/2 teaspoon pepper
1 (10-ounce) can cream of celery soup
1/2 cup chopped onion
2 cups sour cream
1 cup shredded sharp Cheddar cheese
Crushed cornflakes, Italian bread crumbs or butter cracker crumbs
1/4 cup (1/2 stick) margarine

Combine the hash brown potatoes, 1/2 cup margarine, salt, pepper, soup, onion, sour cream and Cheddar cheese in a large bowl and mix well. Place in a buttered 9×13-inch baking dish. Bake at 350 degrees for 30 minutes. Sprinkle with the cornflakes and dot with 1/4 cup margarine. Bake for 30 minutes or until the top is golden brown.

Serves 12

Squash Soufflé

3 pounds yellow squash, sliced
1/2 cup chopped Vidalia onion
1/2 cup cracker meal or bread
    crumbs
2 eggs
1/4 cup (1/2 stick) butter

1 tablespoon sugar
1 teaspoon salt
1/2 teaspoon pepper
1/4 cup (1/2 stick) butter, melted
Bread crumbs

Place the squash in a large saucepan and cover with water. Bring to a boil. Boil until tender; drain. Mash the squash. Add the onion, cracker meal, eggs, 1/4 cup butter, sugar, salt and pepper and mix well. Spoon into a baking dish. Drizzle 1/4 cup butter over the top. Sprinkle with bread crumbs. Bake at 375 degrees for 1 hour or until golden brown.

Serves 8

Sweet Potato Soufflé

3 cups chopped cooked sweet
    potatoes
1 cup sugar
2 eggs
1/2 cup milk
1/2 teaspoon salt

1 teaspoon vanilla extract
1 cup packed brown sugar
1/2 cup flour
1 cup pecans, chopped
1/4 cup (1/2 stick) butter

Combine the sweet potatoes, sugar, eggs, milk, salt and vanilla in a large mixing bowl and beat until smooth. Pour into a buttered 2 1/2-quart baking dish. Combine the brown sugar, flour and pecans in a medium bowl. Cut in the butter until crumbly. Spread evenly over the sweet potato mixture. Bake at 375 degrees for 30 to 40 minutes or until the top is brown.

Serves 8

Selecting Sweet Potatoes and Carrots

Add "orange" to your menu color palette with these two vegetables. Both are high in fiber and nutrients. When selecting fresh sweet potatoes, look for smooth, bright-colored skin without blemishes. Do not store uncooked sweet potatoes in the refrigerator, since the cool temperature will cause the potatoes to turn black and lose their flavor. The best carrots are smooth, slender, and young. The darker the color, the higher the amount of vitamin A. Cut carrots equally so they will cook evenly. The more cutting you do, the more nutrients are lost during cooking.

Both vegetables are high in fiber and nutrients.

Orange-Glazed Sweet Potatoes

4 pounds sweet potatoes or yams
1 cup packed brown sugar
$^1/_2$ cup orange juice
1 tablespoon butter

Rinse the sweet potatoes and place in a large Dutch oven. Cover with water.
Bring to a boil over medium-high heat. Cook, covered, for 30 to 45 minutes or
until tender but not soft; drain and cool. Peel the sweet potatoes and cut into
serving-size pieces. Place in a buttered 2$^1/_2$-quart or 9×13-inch glass baking dish.
Combine the brown sugar, orange juice and butter in a saucepan. Cook over
medium heat for 5 minutes or until clear. Pour over the sweet potatoes. Bake at
350 degrees for 30 minutes, basting with the sauce several times.

Serves 10 to 12

*Note: This is a great make-ahead dish. It can be made one day ahead, covered, chilled, and
reheated in the oven or microwave.*

Fried Green Tomatoes

4 medium green tomatoes
$^1/_2$ cup yellow cornmeal
1 teaspoon dry mustard
Salt and freshly ground pepper to taste
$^1/_4$ cup olive oil
2 bunches arugula leaves, rinsed, patted dry

Cut the tomatoes into slices $^1/_4$ inch thick. Mix the cornmeal, dry mustard,
salt and pepper in a shallow dish. Dip both sides of the tomato slices into the
cornmeal mixture. Place on a large plate. Heat 2 tablespoons of the olive oil in
a large nonstick skillet over medium heat. Add $^1/_2$ of the tomato slices. Cook for
2 to 3 minutes on each side or until golden brown. Remove to a platter to keep
warm. Repeat the process with the remaining 2 tablespoons olive oil and tomatoes.

To serve, line 4 serving plates with the arugula leaves and top with the
fried tomatoes.

Serves 4

Summer Vegetable Bake

3 cups herb-seasoned
    stuffing mix
$1/4$ cup ($1/2$ stick) butter, melted
1 (10-ounce) can cream of
    mushroom soup or cream of
    chicken soup
$1/2$ cup sour cream

$1/2$ cup shredded sharp Cheddar
    cheese
2 cups each shredded yellow
    squash and shredded zucchini
$1/4$ cup shredded carrot
$1/4$ cup finely chopped onion

Mix the stuffing mix and butter in a bowl. Reserve $1/2$ cup of the stuffing
mixture. Place the remaining stuffing mixture in a 2-quart baking dish.
Combine the soup, sour cream and Cheddar cheese in a large bowl and
mix well. Stir in the squash, zucchini, carrot and onion. Spread over the
stuffing mixture. Sprinkle with the reserved stuffing mixture. Bake at
350 degrees for 40 minutes.

Serves 6 to 8

Devilish Eggs

6 eggs
Salt and pepper to taste
1 teaspoon prepared mustard

1 teaspoon vinegar
3 tablespoons mayonnaise
Dash of paprika

Place the eggs gently in a saucepan. Add enough cold water to cover
the eggs by $1/2$ inch. Cover and bring to a boil slowly. Reduce the heat
to low. Cook for 20 minutes. Place the saucepan in the sink and run
cold water over the eggs until cool enough to handle. Tap the eggs on a
cutting board and remove the shell. Cut each egg into halves lengthwise.
Remove the yolks carefully and place in a small bowl. Mash the egg yolks
with a fork. Add salt, pepper, mustard, vinegar and mayonnaise and mix
well. Spoon the egg yolk mixture carefully into the egg whites. Sprinkle
the tops with paprika. Place in a single layer on a serving dish or on a
deviled egg plate. Chill, covered, until ready to serve.

Makes 12

Southern Corn Bread Dressing

1/2 cup (1 stick) butter, melted
1 medium onion, finely chopped
1 cup finely chopped celery
1 tablespoon sage or poultry
   seasoning
1 teaspoon salt
1 teaspoon pepper

4 cups milk
4 cups chicken broth
6 eggs
6 cups crumbled yellow corn bread
4 cups crumbled toasted dried white
   bread

Heat the butter in a skillet over low heat until melted. Add the onion, celery, sage, salt and pepper. Sauté until the onion and celery are transparent. Stir in the milk and broth. Beat the eggs in a large mixing bowl until frothy. Add the corn bread and white bread and mix well. Add the onion mixture and mix well. The mixture should be the consistency of thick soup, which will result in a very moist dressing. Spoon into a greased 9×13-inch baking dish. Bake, covered, at 350 degrees for 1 hour.

Serves 18 to 20

Note: By using the milk and chicken broth you do not have to wait for the turkey to cook to get stock. This also makes a delicious stuffing.

Home-Style Macaroni and Cheese

1 (7-ounce) package elbow macaroni
1/4 cup (1/2 stick) butter
3 tablespoons flour
2 cups milk
8 ounces cream cheese, softened

1 tablespoon Dijon mustard
Salt and pepper to taste
8 ounces sharp Cheddar cheese,
   shredded
2 tablespoons parsley, chopped

1/2 onion/diced bive, sauteed in butter

Cook the macaroni using the package directions; drain. Melt the butter in a large saucepan over medium heat. Stir in the flour. Cook until smooth and bubbly, stirring constantly. Stir in the milk, cream cheese, Dijon mustard, salt and pepper. Cook for 3 minutes or until thickened, stirring constantly. Stir in the macaroni and Cheddar cheese. Spoon into a 2 1/2-quart baking dish sprayed with nonstick cooking spray. Sprinkle with the parsley. Bake at 400 degrees for 20 minutes or until golden brown.

Serves 6 to 8

Garlic Cheese Grits Soufflé

2 tablespoons butter or
   margarine
2 garlic cloves, minced
4 cups water
3/4 teaspoon salt
1/2 teaspoon pepper
1/4 teaspoon dry mustard
1/4 teaspoon turmeric

1 cup uncooked regular grits
4 egg yolks
2 cups shredded sharp Cheddar
   cheese
1/8 teaspoon hot sauce
4 egg whites
1/4 teaspoon cream of tartar
Paprika to taste

Melt the butter in a medium saucepan over medium heat. Add the garlic. Sauté until tender. Stir in the water, salt, pepper, dry mustard and turmeric. Bring to a boil. Stir in the grits gradually. Reduce the heat. Simmer for 15 to 20 minutes or until thickened, stirring occasionally. Remove from the heat. Stir in the egg yolks, Cheddar cheese and hot sauce. Beat the egg whites and cream of tartar at high speed in a large mixing bowl until stiff peaks form. Fold 1/4 of the egg white mixture into the grits. Fold the grits into the remaining egg whites. Pour into a greased and floured 2-quart soufflé dish. Sprinkle with paprika. Bake at 400 degrees for 45 minutes or until puffed and light brown.

Serves 6

✳ Browned Rice

1 cup uncooked rice
1/2 cup (1 stick) margarine
1 (10-ounce) can consommé

1 (10-ounce) can onion soup
1/2 cup sliced mushrooms

Brown the rice in the margarine in a medium saucepan over medium heat. Add the consommé, onion soup and mushrooms and mix well. Pour into a medium baking dish. Bake, covered, at 350 degrees for 1 hour.

Serves 4

Southern Comfort

Nothing says comfort food in the South like steaming corn bread hot from the oven or creamy, buttery grits. Plain or fancy, sweet or savory, these are two pantry staples you can depend on to round out a meal and give it a true southern accent. Grits and corn bread can take the place of mashed potatoes, rice, or noodles in almost any menu. Add vanilla extract, crushed pineapple, maple syrup, or sugar to give grits or corn bread a sweet taste. Add savory flavor by using garlic, garlic and herb cheese, feta or Cheddar cheese, processed cheese, sautéed mushrooms, green onions, chives, or rosemary.

Grits and corn bread can take the place of mashed potatoes, rice, or noodles in almost any menu.

St. Paul's Rice

1 pound pork sausage, crumbled
1 large green bell pepper, chopped
1 large onion, chopped
3 ribs celery, chopped
1 large envelope chicken noodle soup mix
4$\frac{1}{2}$ cups water
$\frac{1}{2}$ cup uncooked rice
1 cup grated cheese (optional)
$\frac{1}{2}$ cup slivered almonds, toasted (optional)

Brown the sausage with the bell pepper, onion and celery in a large skillet, stirring until the sausage is crumbly; drain. Combine the soup mix and water in a large saucepan. Bring to a boil. Cook for 2 minutes. Stir in the sausage mixture and rice. Place in a 2-quart baking dish. Sprinkle with the cheese and almonds. Bake, tightly covered, at 350 degrees for 1 hour.

Serves 8 to 10

Apple Cranberry Casserole

3 cups sliced apples
1 cup cranberries
1 cup sugar
1 cup uncooked rolled oats
3 tablespoons flour
1 cup packed brown sugar
$\frac{1}{2}$ cup (1 stick) butter, melted
1 cup pecans, chopped

Combine the apples, cranberries and sugar in a bowl and toss to coat. Place in a 2-quart baking dish lightly sprayed with nonstick cooking spray. Combine the oats, flour, brown sugar, butter and pecans in a bowl and stir to mix well. Spoon over the fruit mixture. Bake, uncovered, at 350 degrees for 45 minutes.

Serves 8

Note: Serve as a side dish with pork or turkey, or serve as a dessert with vanilla ice cream.

Curried Fruit

1 (28-ounce) can peach halves, drained
1 (16-ounce) can apricot halves, drained
1 (28-ounce) can pear halves, drained
1 (16-ounce) can pineapple slices, drained
1/3 cup butter or margarine
3/4 cup packed light brown sugar
1 teaspoon cinnamon
1 teaspoon curry powder

Layer the peach halves, apricot halves, pear halves and pineapple slices in the order listed in a 3-quart baking dish. Melt the butter, brown sugar, cinnamon and curry powder in a saucepan over low heat. Spoon over the fruit. Bake at 325 degrees for 1 hour. Chill, covered, in the refrigerator for 8 to 12 hours. Bake at 350 degrees for 30 minutes. Serve warm.

Serves 6 to 8

Baked Oranges

6 oranges
6 apples, peeled, cored, chopped
1 (8-ounce) can crushed pineapple
1 cup sugar
1/4 cup (1/2 stick) butter or margarine
1/4 cup packed brown sugar
1/4 cup pecan halves

Cut the oranges into halves and discard the seeds. Scoop the pulp and orange juice into a Dutch oven, reserving the orange shells. Add the apples, pineapple and sugar. Cook over medium heat for 30 minutes or until the mixture is reduced, stirring frequently. Spoon into the reserved orange shells on a baking sheet. Dot each with the butter. Sprinkle with the brown sugar. Top with the pecan halves. Bake at 375 degrees for 15 to 20 minutes or until heated through.

Serves 12

STAR House Builds Bright Futures

In 1993, the JLGNF chose two focus areas in which to further concentrate its community efforts: Children at Risk and Homelessness. As part of this directive, the League founded STAR House, an after-school mentoring and enrichment program for at-risk children in Roswell.

Its purpose was to provide the children a challenging curriculum to integrate the basic principles of education by "Seeking, Teaching, and Reaching." Children ages six to fourteen have access to a computer lab, library, arts and crafts room, and classroom-style rooms used for homework and tutoring. There is a strong emphasis on reading and phonics.

Today, STAR House stands on its own as The STAR House Foundation, with its own board of directors, support from local agencies, and a second location.

Pineapple Casserole

2 (20-ounce) cans crushed pineapple
1 cup sugar
6 tablespoons flour
2 cups shredded Cheddar cheese
1/2 cup (1 stick) butter, melted
1 cup crushed butter crackers

Drain the pineapple, reserving 6 tablespoons of the juice. Mix the reserved pineapple juice, sugar and flour in a bowl until smooth. Pour into a 9×13-inch glass baking dish. Layer the pineapple and cheese over the mixture. Mix the butter and cracker crumbs in a bowl. Sprinkle over the cheese layer. Bake at 350 degrees for 25 to 30 minutes or until bubbly.

Serves 12

Corn, Tomato and Basil Relish

6 large ears white corn
2 tablespoons olive oil
1 tablespoon finely chopped garlic
1/2 cup fresh basil, chopped
5 plum tomatoes, seeded, chopped
3 tablespoons balsamic vinegar
Salt and pepper to taste

Husk the corn and remove the silks. Cut the kernels from the cobs into a bowl using a large knife. Heat the olive oil in a large heavy skillet over medium-high heat. Add the garlic. Sauté for 1 minute. Add the corn. Sauté for 5 minutes. Remove from the heat. Stir in 1/2 of the basil. Spoon into a large bowl. Stir in the tomatoes and balsamic vinegar. Season lightly with salt and pepper. Chill, covered, for 3 hours or longer. Sprinkle with the remaining basil before serving.

Serves 6

Caribbean Salsa

1 cantaloupe, diced
1 Vidalia onion, chopped
1/2 cup red wine vinegar
1/4 cup olive oil
Chopped fresh cilantro to taste

Combine the cantaloupe, Vidalia onion, red wine vinegar, olive oil and cilantro in a bowl. Chill, covered, for several hours before serving.

Makes 8 cups

Note: Serve as a side dish with any meat or omelet, or serve as an appetizer with tortilla chips.

Mango Salsa

1 mango, diced
2 jalapeños, seeded, chopped
Zest and juice of 2 limes
Chopped red onion to taste
1/2 bunch cilantro, chopped
2 tablespoons extra-virgin olive oil
Salt and pepper to taste

Combine the mango, jalapeños, lime zest, lime juice, red onion, cilantro, olive oil and salt and pepper in a bowl and mix well. Chill, covered, until ready to serve.

Makes 2 cups

Note: Excellent served with grilled pork or fish. Be sure to use rubber gloves when handling the jalapeños.

A View from the Kids' Table

Many adults' first Thanksgiving memory is of a rickety card table in the corner and a paper plate full of dark turkey meat and mashed potatoes. Bring your children into the spirit of the day by letting them decorate your table. Make turkey place cards with pinecones you find in your yard. Use colorful construction paper for the turkey's head and feathers. Scatter colorful autumn leaves, acorns, and other yard treasures around the table. Older friends and family love seeing children's handiwork and the activity will keep young ones busy and out of the kitchen.

Make turkey place cards with pinecones you find in your yard.

Lawrenceville

The Gwinnett County center of government features a beautiful old courthouse that showcases the town's best of old and new. With the gleaming red building as its centerpiece, downtown Lawrenceville has begun a restoration. New industry plus a friendly atmosphere makes Lawrenceville attractive to newcomers.

The city was named for James Lawrence, captain of the U.S. frigate CHESAPEAKE, and was the first town chartered in Gwinnett County. Lawrenceville was incorporated in 1821, and the city began to grow up around the courthouse. The streets radiating from the square were named for judges, war heroes, and native trees.

The historic courthouse is home to several festivals, including the Holiday Lighting of the Courthouse, arts festivals, and the outdoor Brown Bag Concert Series. The building itself is on the National Register of Historic Places. Inside, the Gwinnett History Center and Historical Society provides genealogical research and keeps archives of Gwinnett County's past. The Gwinnett History Museum, also in Lawrenceville, was built in 1855 as the Lawrenceville Female Seminary.

Desserts

Piña Colada Cheesecake

1²/₃ cups graham cracker crumbs
¹/₄ cup sugar
¹/₂ cup (1 stick) butter or margarine, melted
32 ounces cream cheese, softened
³/₄ cup sugar
4 eggs
1 cup sour cream
1 (15-ounce) can cream of coconut
1 (15-ounce) can crushed pineapple
2 tablespoons cornstarch
1 teaspoon vanilla extract
1 teaspoon rum flavoring
1 teaspoon lemon juice
¹/₄ cup (¹/₂ stick) butter or margarine
¹/₂ cup flaked coconut
¹/₂ cup almonds, chopped
¹/₄ cup sugar

For the crust, combine the graham cracker crumbs, ¹/₄ cup sugar and ¹/₂ cup butter in a bowl and mix well. Press over the bottom of a 10-inch springform pan. Bake at 350 degrees for 10 minutes. Remove from the oven to cool.

For the filling, beat the cream cheese in a large mixing bowl until smooth. Add ³/₄ cup sugar and beat well. Add the eggs 1 at a time, beating well after each addition. Stir in the sour cream, cream of coconut, pineapple, cornstarch, vanilla, rum flavoring and lemon juice. Spoon into the cooled crust. Bake at 350 degrees for 1 hour and 20 minutes; turn off the oven.

For the topping, combine ¹/₄ cup butter, coconut, almonds and ¹/₄ cup sugar in a small saucepan. Cook over low heat until the sugar dissolves, stirring constantly. Remove the cheesecake from the oven. Sprinkle the topping over the top of the cheesecake. Return to the oven and close the oven door. Let stand for 1 hour. Remove the cheesecake from the oven. Chill, covered, until ready to serve.

Serves 10 to 12

White Chocolate Cheesecake

1/2 cup (1 stick) butter, melted
2 cups Lorna Doone cookies, finely ground
1 ounce white chocolate, grated
32 ounces cream cheese, softened
1 1/4 cups sugar
Pinch of salt
4 eggs
3 ounces white chocolate, grated
2 cups sour cream
1/4 cup sugar
1 teaspoon vanilla extract
1 ounce white chocolate, shaved

For the crust, combine the butter, cookie crumbs and 1 ounce white chocolate in a bowl. Press into a 10-inch springform pan.

For the cheesecake, beat the cream cheese and 1 1/4 cups sugar in a mixing bowl until fluffy. Add the salt and mix well. Add the eggs 1 at a time, beating well at low speed after each addition. Stir in 3 ounces white chocolate. Spoon into the prepared pan. Bake at 350 degrees for 40 to 45 minutes. Remove from the oven. Cool for 10 minutes.

For the topping, combine the sour cream, 1/4 cup sugar and vanilla in a small bowl and mix well. Spread over the cheesecake. Return to the oven. Bake for 10 minutes. Cover and refrigerate immediately. Sprinkle with 1 ounce white chocolate before serving.

Serves 10

From the Wine List

There's nothing like a taste of something sweet to give a grand finale to any good meal. Whether you use a fork or a glass to savor the sweetness is up to you! Dessert wines are fruity—like the raspberry-flavored Vin du Framboise from Bonny Doon (ask for it at a reliable wine retailer). Try it over vanilla bean ice cream. Moscato d'asti is a white dessert wine with peachy, melony flavors. Any wine identified as a dessert wine is sweetly satisfying. Serving dessert wines alone after a meal lets your company enjoy the complex flavors and satisfies the sweetest tooth with a minimum of fuss and fat grams.

Any wine identified as a dessert wine is sweetly satisfying.

Peach Berry Upside-Down Crisp

1 pound frozen unsweetened sliced peaches, thawed
2 cups fresh blueberries, or 8 ounces frozen blueberries, thawed
1/2 cup sugar
1 cup flour
1/2 cup sugar
1/2 cup old-fashioned oats
1/2 cup milk
1 teaspoon vanilla extract
1/2 cup (1 stick) unsalted butter, melted, cooled

Combine the peaches, blueberries and 1/2 cup sugar in a bowl and toss to coat. Let stand for 15 minutes. Combine the flour, 1/2 cup sugar, oats, milk and vanilla in a bowl and mix well. Stir in the butter. The batter will be thick. Spread in a 9×13-inch glass baking dish. Spoon the fruit mixture over the top. Bake at 400 degrees for 45 minutes or until cooked through and the bottom is brown. Let stand for 10 minutes. Serve warm with ice cream.

Serves 8 to 10

Quick and Easy Banana Pudding

1 (6-ounce) package vanilla instant pudding mix
2 1/2 cups milk
1 cup sour cream
12 ounces whipped topping
1 (16-ounce) package vanilla wafers
5 or 6 bananas, sliced vertically
Garnish: Crushed vanilla wafers

Combine the pudding mix, milk and sour cream in a mixing bowl and beat until thickened. Fold in 1/2 of the whipped topping. Alternate layers of vanilla wafers, bananas and pudding mixture in a trifle bowl until all of the ingredients are used. Top with the remaining whipped topping. Garnish with crushed vanilla wafers. Chill, covered, until ready to serve.

Serves 10 to 12

Bread Pudding with Vanilla Sauce

6 slices dried bread, cut into $1/2$-inch cubes
1 cup hot water
1 cup packed brown sugar
4 eggs, lightly beaten
2 cups warm milk
$1/2$ cup sugar
$1/2$ teaspoon vanilla extract
$1/2$ teaspoon cinnamon
$1/8$ teaspoon salt
Vanilla Sauce (below)

Place the bread in a greased 2-quart baking dish. Mix the hot water and brown sugar in a bowl. Pour over the bread. Combine the eggs, milk, sugar, vanilla, cinnamon and salt in a bowl and mix well. Pour over the top. Bake at 350 degrees for 50 to 60 minutes or until a knife inserted in the center comes out clean. Drizzle with Vanilla Sauce.

Serves 8

Note: You may serve this bread pudding warm or cold.

Vanilla Sauce

2 tablespoons sugar
1 tablespoon cornstarch
3 tablespoons butter
$3/4$ cup milk
$1/4$ cup light corn syrup
1 teaspoon vanilla extract

Mix the sugar and cornstarch together. Melt the butter in a saucepan over low heat. Stir in the sugar mixture. Add the milk and corn syrup and stir to mix well. Bring to a boil over medium heat. Boil for 1 minute. Remove from the heat. Stir in the vanilla. Serve warm.

Makes $1^1/4$ cups

Chocolate Bread Pudding with Godiva Cream

5 cups diced white bread
1 cup (6 ounces) semisweet
   chocolate chips
3 cups warm milk
3 tablespoons Godiva liqueur
3 egg yolks

$^1/_3$ cup sugar
$^1/_2$ teaspoon cinnamon
$^1/_4$ teaspoon salt
1 teaspoon vanilla extract
2 cups whipping cream
$^1/_4$ cup Godiva liqueur

Combine the bread, chocolate chips, milk and 3 tablespoons Godiva liqueur in a large bowl. Let stand for 15 minutes. Mix the egg yolks, sugar, cinnamon, salt and vanilla in a bowl. Add to the bread mixture and stir with a fork until blended. Pour into a greased 2-quart baking dish. Set the dish in a larger pan of hot water. Bake at 350 degrees for 45 minutes. Beat the whipping cream in a bowl until thick. Add $^1/_4$ cup Godiva liqueur and beat until stiff peaks form. Serve over the warm pudding.

Serves 6 to 8

Nutty Cream Cheese Delight

1 cup flour
$^1/_2$ cup (1 stick) butter, softened
$^3/_4$ cup chopped nuts
8 ounces cream cheese, softened
1 cup confectioners' sugar

8 ounces whipped topping
2 (4-ounce) packages any flavor
   instant pudding mix
3 cups milk
$^1/_4$ cup chopped nuts

Mix the flour, butter and $^3/_4$ cup nuts in a bowl. Press in a 9×13-inch baking dish. Bake at 325 degrees for 25 minutes. Let stand until cool. Beat the cream cheese and confectioners' sugar in a mixing bowl until smooth. Fold in 1 cup of the whipped topping. Spread over the cooled pastry. Beat the pudding mix and milk in a bowl until thick. Spread over the cream cheese mixture. Chill, covered, for 8 to 12 hours or until set. Spread the remaining whipped topping over the top. Sprinkle with $^1/_4$ cup nuts.

Serves 12

Coffee Charlotte

2 envelopes unflavored gelatin
2 tablespoons cold water
2 tablespoons instant coffee
  powder
2/3 cup sugar
1/4 teaspoon salt

3 cups milk
1/4 cup Cognac
2 cups whipping cream, whipped
12 ladyfingers, split
Garnish: Grated semisweet
  chocolate

Soften the gelatin in 2 tablespoons cold water. Combine the softened gelatin, coffee powder, sugar and salt in a saucepan. Stir in the milk. Cook over low heat until the sugar and gelatin are dissolved, stirring constantly. Remove from the heat. Stir in the Cognac. Chill until the mixture mounds slightly when dropped from a spoon. Fold in the whipped cream. Line a springform pan with ladyfingers. Pour in the coffee mixture. Chill for 8 to 12 hours or until firm. Remove the side of the springform pan. Garnish with grated semisweet chocolate.

Serves 10

Punch Bowl Cake

1 (2-layer) package yellow
  cake mix
1 (6-ounce) package vanilla
  instant pudding mix
5 cups milk
16 ounces whipped topping
1 cup pecans, chopped

2 (16-ounce) cans cherry or
  strawberry pie filling
2 (16-ounce) cans crushed
  pineapple, drained
5 large bananas, sliced
Garnish: Maraschino cherries or
  fresh strawberries

Prepare and bake the cake mix using the package directions for a 9×13-inch cake pan or 2 round 9-inch cake pans. Let stand until cool. Crumble the cake. Mix the pudding mix and milk in a bowl until thick. Mix the whipped topping and pecans in a bowl. Layer the cake, pudding mixture, cherry pie filling, pineapple, bananas and whipped topping mixture 1/2 at a time in a crystal punch bowl or trifle bowl. Chill, covered, for 4 hours or longer. Garnish with maraschino cherries before serving.

Serves 24

Baking with Ladyfingers

Two types of cookies or cakes share the name ladyfingers. The first is a delicate, fine-textured biscuit that is rectangular-shaped. They are most commonly used in creating crusts for desserts by grinding into a powder or layering side by side. Ladyfinger biscuits are used primarily in tiramisus and trifles and can be found in the Italian food section of most supermarkets. The second type of ladyfinger is a sponge-like rectangular cake. Their texture lends their use to recipes for puddings and cakes. You can find these in your supermarket's bakery section.

Two types of cookies or cakes share the name ladyfingers.

Tiramisu

6 egg yolks
1¼ cups sugar
1¼ cups mascarpone cheese
1 teaspoon vanilla extract
1¾ cups whipping cream, whipped
2 packages ladyfingers, split
⅓ cup Kahlúa or coffee liqueur
Garnishes: Baking cocoa, whipped cream and chocolate syrup

Beat the egg yolks and sugar in a mixing bowl until thick and pale yellow. Pour into a double boiler over boiling water. Reduce the heat to low. Cook for 8 to 10 minutes or until smooth and thickened, stirring constantly. Remove from the heat. Beat in the mascarpone cheese and vanilla. Cool. Fold in the whipped cream.

To assemble, line the bottom of a dish with ladyfingers. Brush with ½ of the liqueur. Spoon ½ of the cream mixture over the ladyfingers. Layer the remaining ladyfingers over the cream mixture. Brush with the remaining liqueur. Spread with the remaining cream mixture. Garnish with baking cocoa. Chill, covered, for 3 to 12 hours.

To serve, cut into squares and place on dessert plates. Garnish each serving with a dollop of whipped cream and a drizzle of chocolate syrup.

Serves 10 to 12

Mocha Fudge Ice Cream Torte

1 1/2 cups Oreo cookie crumbs
2 tablespoons butter, melted
1 quart chocolate ice cream

1/2 cup chocolate sauce
1 quart coffee ice cream
1 (4-ounce) toffee bar, crushed

Mix the cookie crumbs and butter in a bowl. Press into a 9-inch springform pan. Bake at 350 degrees for 8 to 10 minutes. Let stand until cool. Spread the chocolate ice cream over the cooled crust. Drizzle with 1/2 of the chocolate sauce. Freeze until firm. Spread with the coffee ice cream. Sprinkle with the crushed candy. Drizzle with the remaining chocolate sauce. Cover with plastic wrap. Freeze until firm. Store in the freezer.

Serves 10

Chocolate Toffee Trifle

1 (2-layer) package devil's food
   cake mix or brownie mix
6 ounces Heath bars, frozen
1 1/2 cups milk

1/2 cup Kahlúa
16 ounces whipped topping
1 (4-ounce) package chocolate
   instant pudding mix

Prepare and bake the cake mix using the package directions for a 9×13-inch cake pan. Let stand until cool. Cut the cake into 1-inch cubes. Place the unwrapped candy bars in a sealable heavy-duty plastic bag. Seal the bag and crush the candy bars with a hammer. Combine the milk, Kahlúa and pudding mix in a mixing bowl and beat until thick.

To assemble, layer the cake, pudding mixture, whipped topping and crushed candy bars 1/2 at a time in a large glass bowl. Chill, covered, for 8 to 12 hours before serving.

Serves 8 to 10

Trifling with Delicious Desserts

A trifle is a simple way to use "yesterday's cake." Leftover pound cake or angel food cake makes the perfect trifle when cut into bite-size cubes and soaked with a liqueur. Make an ordinary brownie or cake made from a mix take on new life when presented this way. Layer the cake in a special trifle bowl and alternate with a custard or flavored cream. Cover and refrigerate for at least four hours. Voila! You have transformed leftover cake into a lovely new dessert. You also can add flavored whipped cream (maybe with a bit of rum), fresh fruit, berries, ice cream, nuts, and other liqueurs.

A trifle is a simple way to use "yesterday's cake."

Peach Trifle

1 prepared angel food cake
1/4 cup orange juice
2 cups cold milk
1 (4-ounce) package vanilla instant pudding mix
13 ounces whipped topping
3 fresh peaches, sliced, chopped

Cut the cake horizontally into 3 layers. Sprinkle the cake evenly with orange juice. Cut into 1-inch cubes. Combine the milk and pudding mix in a medium bowl. Beat for 30 seconds with a whisk. Let stand for 2 minutes or until thickened. Fold in 2 cups of the whipped topping.

To assemble, layer the cake cubes, peaches and pudding mixture 1/2 at a time in a 2 1/2-quart trifle dish or glass bowl. Garnish with the remaining whipped topping. Chill, covered, for 1 hour before serving.

Serves 8 to 10

Note: Using fat-free and sugar-free ingredients does not compromise this recipe.

Spiced Pears

3 (16-ounce) cans sliced pears in syrup
1 cup packed light brown sugar
1/2 teaspoon cinnamon
1/4 teaspoon nutmeg
1/4 teaspoon allspice
1/4 cup lemon juice or orange juice

Drain the pears, reserving 1 cup of the syrup. Combine the reserved syrup, brown sugar, cinnamon, nutmeg, allspice and orange juice in a large bowl and mix well. Add the pears and mix gently to cover the pears with the syrup. Macerate, covered, in the refrigerator for 8 to 48 hours.

Serves 12

Chunky Carrot Cakes

2 cups flour
2 cups sugar
1 teaspoon salt
1 teaspoon baking powder
1 teaspoon baking soda
4 teaspoons cinnamon
1 teaspoon nutmeg
1¼ cups vegetable oil

4 eggs
2 cups shredded carrots
1 cup shredded coconut
1 cup golden raisins or drained
   crushed pineapple
1 cup pecans, chopped
Cream Cheese Frosting (below)

Mix the flour, sugar, salt, baking powder, baking soda, cinnamon and nutmeg in a large mixing bowl. Add the oil. Add the eggs 1 at a time, beating well after each addition. Stir in the carrots, coconut, raisins and pecans. Pour equal amounts into 3 medium loaf pans sprayed with nonstick cooking spray. Bake at 350 degrees for 40 minutes or until a wooden pick inserted in the center comes out clean. Cool in the pans for 10 minutes. Remove to wire racks to cool completely. Spread Cream Cheese Frosting on top of each loaf.

Serves 12

Note: This recipe can be made into a traditional layer cake by baking the batter in 3 greased and floured 9-inch round cake pans and doubling the frosting recipe.

Cream Cheese Frosting

¼ cup (½ stick) butter,
   softened
4 ounces cream cheese, softened

2 cups confectioners' sugar
   (8 ounces)
1 teaspoon vanilla extract

Beat the butter and cream cheese in a mixing bowl until light and fluffy. Add the confectioners' sugar and vanilla and beat until smooth.

Makes 3 cups

Chocolate Cola Cake

1 (2-layer) package devil's food cake mix without pudding
1 (4-ounce) package chocolate instant pudding mix
4 eggs
$^1/_2$ cup vegetable oil
$1^1/_4$ cups cola
Chocolate Cola Frosting (below)

Combine the cake mix, pudding mix, eggs and oil in a large mixing bowl. Beat at low speed until blended. Bring the cola to a boil in a small saucepan over medium heat. Add to the batter gradually, beating constantly. Beat at medium speed for 2 minutes. Pour into a greased and floured 9×13-inch cake pan. Bake at 350 degrees for 30 minutes or until a wooden pick inserted in the center comes out clean. Cool on a wire rack for 10 minutes. Spread warm Chocolate Cola Frosting over the warm cake. Let cool completely before cutting.

Serves 15

Note: As residents of a suburb of Atlanta, of course we used Coca-Cola for testing this recipe. You may also use German chocolate cake mix instead of devil's food cake mix with equally delicious results.

Chocolate Cola Frosting

$^1/_2$ cup (1 stick) butter or margarine
$^1/_4$ cup plus 2 tablespoons cola
3 tablespoons baking cocoa
1 (1-pound) package confectioners' sugar
1 teaspoon vanilla extract
1 cup chopped pecans, toasted

Combine the butter, cola and baking cocoa in a medium saucepan. Cook over medium heat until the butter melts, stirring constantly. Do not boil. Remove from the heat. Add the confectioners' sugar and vanilla and stir until smooth. Stir in the pecans.

Make 4 cups

Chocolate Chip Cake

1 (2-layer) package yellow
    cake mix
1 (6-ounce) package chocolate
    instant pudding mix
2 cups sour cream

3/4 cup vegetable or corn oil
4 eggs
2 cups (12 ounces) chocolate
    chips
Confectioners' sugar

Combine the cake mix, pudding mix, sour cream, oil and eggs in a large
mixing bowl and beat until smooth. Stir in the chocolate chips. Pour
into a greased and floured bundt pan. Bake at 350 degrees for 1 hour.
Cool in the pan on a wire rack. Invert onto a cake plate. Sprinkle with
confectioners' sugar.

Serves 16

Variation: Substitute 1 cup peanut butter chips for 1 cup of the chocolate chips.

European Chocolate Cake

1 (2-layer) package devil's food
    cake mix without pudding
3 eggs
1/2 cup vegetable oil
1 1/3 cups water
1/2 cup heavy cream

1 cup (6 ounces) semisweet
    chocolate chips
1 cup seedless raspberry jam
Garnishes: Whipped cream and
    fresh raspberries

Combine the cake mix, eggs, oil and water in a large mixing bowl. Beat
at medium speed for 2 minutes. Spoon into 3 greased and floured 8-inch
round cake pans. Bake at 350 degrees for 18 minutes or until layers test
done. Cool in the pans for 10 minutes. Invert onto wire racks to cool
completely. Microwave the cream on High in a microwave-safe bowl for
1 minute. Add the chocolate chips and stir until smooth. Let stand for
1 minute or until the mixture becomes thick.

To assemble, spread the raspberry jam between the cake layers. Spread
the chocolate icing over the top and side of the cake. Garnish with
whipped cream and fresh raspberries.

Serves 10 to 12

Chocolate Drizzle Cake

1 cup (2 sticks) butter or margarine, softened
1½ cups sugar
4 eggs
½ teaspoon baking soda
1 cup buttermilk
2½ cups flour
1 cup (6 ounces) semisweet chocolate chips
2 (4-ounce) bars sweet baking chocolate, melted, cooled
⅓ cup chocolate syrup
2 teaspoons vanilla extract
4 ounces white chocolate, chopped
2 tablespoons shortening
½ cup (3 ounces) semisweet chocolate chips
2 teaspoons shortening

Beat the butter in a large mixing bowl until creamy. Add the sugar gradually, beating constantly at medium speed. Add the eggs 1 at a time, beating well after each addition. Dissolve the baking soda in the buttermilk. Add the flour and buttermilk mixture alternately to the creamed mixture, beating well after each addition and beginning and ending with the flour. Add 1 cup chocolate chips, melted chocolate, chocolate syrup and vanilla and stir just until blended. Do not overbeat. Spoon into a greased and floured 10-inch bundt pan.

Bake at 300 degrees for 1 hour and 25 minutes to 1 hour and 35 minutes or until the cake springs back when lightly touched. Remove from the oven and invert immediately onto a serving plate. Cool completely.

Combine the white chocolate and 2 tablespoons shortening in a double boiler. Cook over simmering water until smooth, stirring constantly. Remove from the heat. Drizzle over the cooled cake. Melt ½ cup chocolate chips and 2 teaspoons shortening in a saucepan over low heat, stirring constantly. Remove from the heat and let cool. Drizzle over the white chocolate.

Serves 15

Almond Pound Cake

3 1/4 cups flour
1/2 teaspoon baking powder
1/2 teaspoon salt
1 cup (2 sticks) butter, softened
1/2 cup shortening

3 cups sugar
5 eggs
1 cup milk
1 teaspoon vanilla extract
1 teaspoon almond extract

Sift the flour, baking powder and salt together. Beat the butter, shortening and sugar in a mixing bowl until light and fluffy. Add the eggs 1 at a time, beating well after each addition. Add the flour mixture and milk alternately to the creamed mixture, beginning and ending with the flour mixture and beating well after each addition. Stir in the flavorings. Pour into a greased and floured bundt pan. Bake at 275 degrees for 2 hours or until a wooden pick inserted in the center comes out clean.

Serves 16

Cream Cheese Pound Cake

1 1/2 cups (3 sticks) butter, softened
3 cups sugar
8 ounces cream cheese, softened
6 eggs

Dash of salt
1 1/2 teaspoons vanilla extract
3 cups cake flour
1 1/2 cups chopped pecans (optional)

Beat the butter, sugar and cream cheese in a mixing bowl until light and fluffy. Add the eggs 1 at a time, beating well after each addition. Add the salt and vanilla. Stir in the cake flour. Sprinkle 1/2 cup of the pecans into a greased and floured tube pan. Stir the remaining pecans into the batter. Pour the batter into the prepared pan. Bake at 325 degrees for 1 1/4 hours.

Serves 16

Bundt and Tube Pans—There is a Difference!

The recipes featured on these pages call for specific cake pans known as bundt and tube pans. The bundt pan has a beveled side, while the side of a tube pan is smooth. Be sure to use the pan specified in each recipe if you want your cake to turn out properly. You can expect the batter to run over the side and the cake to fall out of the pan if the pan is too small; likewise, if the pan is too big, baking time is slowed when the side "shields" the batter. A 10-inch tube pan holds 16 cups of batter and a 10-inch bundt pan holds around 12 cups.

The bundt pan has a beveled side, while the side of a tube pan is smooth.

Red Velvet Cake

4 ounces German's sweet chocolate
$1/2$ cup red food coloring (2 small bottles)
$2^1/2$ cups flour
1 teaspoon baking soda
$1/2$ teaspoon salt
1 cup (2 sticks) butter, softened
2 cups sugar
4 egg yolks
1 teaspoon vanilla extract
1 cup buttermilk
4 egg whites, stiffly beaten
Cream Cheese Frosting (below)

Melt the chocolate with the food coloring in a small saucepan. Sift the flour, baking soda and salt together. Cream the butter and sugar in a mixing bowl until light and fluffy. Add the egg yolks, vanilla and chocolate mixture and mix well. Add the flour mixture alternately with the buttermilk, beating well after each addition. Fold in the egg whites. Pour into 3 greased and floured 9-inch round cake pans. Bake at 350 degrees for 35 minutes or until the layers test done. Cool in the pans for 10 minutes. Invert onto wire racks to cool completely. Spread Cream Cheese Frosting between the layers and over the top and side of the cake.

Serves 12

Cream Cheese Frosting

8 ounces cream cheese, softened
$1/2$ cup (1 stick) butter, softened
1 (1-pound) package confectioners' sugar
1 teaspoon vanilla extract
Milk

Beat the cream cheese, butter, confectioners' sugar and vanilla in a mixing bowl until smooth. Add enough milk 1 tablespoon at a time to make of the desired spreading consistency.

Makes $4^1/2$ cups

Strawberry Jewel Cake

1 (2-layer) package white cake mix
1 (3-ounce) package strawberry gelatin
1 cup vegetable oil
$^1/_2$ cup water
1 cup crushed thawed frozen strawberries
4 eggs
1 cup shredded coconut (optional)
1 cup chopped pecans (optional)
Strawberry Frosting (below)

Combine the cake mix, gelatin, oil, water and strawberries in a mixing bowl and mix until blended. Add the eggs 1 at a time, beating well after each addition. Stir in the coconut and pecans. Pour into 3 greased and floured 9-inch round cake pans. Bake at 350 degrees for 25 to 30 minutes or until the layers test done. Cool in the pans for 10 minutes. Invert onto wire racks to cool completely. Spread Strawberry Frosting between the layers and over the top and side of the cake.

Serves 12

Note: Excess liquid can form when thawing frozen strawberries, so drain when necessary. Fresh strawberries can be used when available.

Strawberry Frosting

1 (1-pound) package confectioners' sugar
$^1/_4$ cup ($^1/_2$ stick) margarine, softened
$^1/_2$ cup crushed thawed frozen strawberries

Combine the confectioners' sugar, margarine and strawberries in a mixing bowl and beat until smooth.

Makes 4$^1/_2$ cups

A Pound of This, a Pound of That

Many a dinner has ended with the flourish of a pound cake. The old-fashioned pound cake recipe (circa 1900) contains one pound each of flour, butter, sugar, and eggs. In the "good old days" before electric appliances, it took two hours to beat the batter by hand! Nowadays, you can cut the mixing time at least in half with a good electric mixer. The pound cake recipes in this chapter are quite a bit easier to prepare. Any pound cake can be served à la mode with your favorite store-bought ice cream. Try cinnamon or peppermint ice cream with chocolate sauce in the winter, or pineapple sherbet in the summer.

The old-fashioned pound cake recipe (circa 1900) contains one pound each of flour, butter, sugar, and eggs.

Strawberry Cream Cake

1 (14-ounce) can sweetened condensed milk
1/3 cup lemon juice
1 teaspoon almond extract
13 ounces whipped topping
1 prepared angel food cake
2 pints fresh strawberries, sliced

Combine the condensed milk, lemon juice and almond extract in a large mixing bowl and stir to mix well. Fold in the whipped topping. Chill for 10 minutes. Cut the cake horizontally into 3 or 4 layers using a long serrated knife. Reserve 5 or 6 strawberry slices. Fold the remaining strawberries into the whipped topping mixture. Spread between the layers and over the top and side of the cake. Spoon any leftover filling into the center of the cake. Garnish with the reserved strawberries.

Serves 16

Note: When fresh strawberries are not available, use one 10-ounce package frozen strawberries, draining away some of the juice.

Caramel Corn

4 packages plain microwave popcorn
1 cup (2 sticks) margarine
1/2 cup white corn syrup
2 cups packed brown sugar
1 teaspoon cream of tartar
1 teaspoon baking soda

Microwave the popcorn using the package directions. Place in a large bowl. Bring the margarine, corn syrup, brown sugar and cream of tartar to a boil in a saucepan. Boil for 5 minutes, stirring constantly. Remove from the heat. Stir in the baking soda. The mixture will foam. Pour over the popcorn. Place in a large greased baking pan. Bake at 250 degrees for 1 hour, stirring every 15 minutes. Spread quickly on a clean surface and cool. Break apart and store in an airtight container.

Makes 16 servings

Chocolate Oatmeal Drops

2 cups sugar
1/2 cup (1 stick) margarine
1/4 cup baking cocoa
1/2 cup milk
1 teaspoon vanilla extract
1/2 cup peanut butter
2 1/2 cups quick-cooking oats

Combine the sugar, margarine, baking cocoa, milk and vanilla in a heavy saucepan. Bring to a boil over medium-high heat, stirring constantly. Boil for 2 minutes. Remove from the heat. Stir in the peanut butter and oats. Drop quickly by tablespoonfuls onto waxed paper. Let stand until cool.

Makes 2 dozen

Peanut Butter Fudge

1 cup (2 sticks) margarine
1 (16-ounce) jar chunky peanut butter
1 (1-pound) package confectioners' sugar
1 teaspoon vanilla extract

Melt the margarine in a saucepan. Stir in the peanut butter. Add the confectioners' sugar gradually, mixing well after each addition. Stir in the vanilla. Cook over medium heat until heated through, stirring constantly. Do not boil. Spread on a baking sheet or in a 9×13-inch glass dish. Cool completely before cutting into bars.

Makes 3 dozen

Crackle Toffee

60 to 70 saltines
1½ cups (3 sticks) butter
1½ cups dark brown sugar
1½ teaspoons vanilla extract
4 cups (24 ounces) semisweet chocolate chips
2½ cups chopped walnuts

Line a 10×15-inch baking pan with foil. Arrange the crackers in a single layer in the prepared pan, breaking the crackers as needed to cover the entire surface. Bring the butter and brown sugar to a boil in a saucepan over medium-high heat. Reduce the heat. Simmer for 3 minutes. Remove from the heat. Add the vanilla. Pour evenly over the crackers. Bake at 400 degrees for 5 minutes. Remove from the oven and turn off the oven. Sprinkle with the chocolate chips and walnuts. Return to the oven. Let stand until the chocolate chips are melted. Spread evenly over the top using a knife or spatula. Let stand until cooled completely. Break into pieces and store in an airtight container.

Makes about 5 dozen

Chocolate Bourbon Truffles

9 ounces chocolate wafers, crushed
8 ounces finely chopped pecans
⅓ cup baking cocoa
¼ cup sugar
½ cup light corn syrup
⅓ cup bourbon
Chocolate sprinkles

Combine the crushed wafers, pecans, baking cocoa and sugar in a large bowl and mix well. Stir in the corn syrup and bourbon. Shape into ³/4-inch balls. Roll in chocolate sprinkles. Place in an airtight container. Store in the refrigerator.

Makes 5 dozen

White Chocolate Crunch

5 cups Crispix
3 cups Cheerios
2 cups broken pretzel sticks
1 cup cocktail peanuts
1 (1-pound) package "M & M's" Chocolate Candies
2 pounds white chocolate (almond bark)

Mix the cereals, pretzel sticks, peanuts and candies in a large bowl. Melt the white chocolate using the package directions. Pour over the cereal mixture and stir with a wooden spoon to coat. Spread on waxed paper. Let stand until set. Break into pieces. Store in an airtight container.

Makes 12 cups

Spiced Pecans

$^1/_2$ cup sugar
$^3/_4$ teaspoon salt
1 teaspoon cinnamon
$^1/_4$ teaspoon cloves
$^1/_4$ teaspoon nutmeg
1 egg white
1 tablespoon water
2 cups pecan halves

Mix the sugar, salt, cinnamon, cloves and nutmeg in a small bowl. Beat the egg white and water in a mixing bowl until soft peaks form. Add the pecan halves and stir to coat. Add the sugar mixture and stir to coat. Spread evenly on a baking sheet sprayed with nonstick cooking spray. Bake at 250 degrees for $1^1/_2$ hours, stirring every 30 minutes.

Makes 2 cups

Note: To add a special touch during the holidays, lightly sprinkle the pecans with gold powder after removing from the oven. Gold powder can be found at cake decorating supply stores.

The Association of Junior Leagues International Inc.

A network of over 290 women's service organizations began with one woman, Mary Harriman, in New York City in 1901. Mary and her friends founded an organization dedicated to "improving the conditions that surround us." A century later, Junior Leagues are found all over the United States, Great Britain, Canada, and Mexico. Some of the more recognizable names of Junior League women include Supreme Court Justice Sandra Day O'Connor, author Eudora Welty, and four First Ladies: Eleanor Roosevelt, Betty Ford, Nancy Reagan, and Barbara Bush. AJLI unites local Leagues and provides training to women who volunteer in their communities. Since cookbooks are one of the more popular ways for Junior Leagues to raise money, the AJLI has printed two cookbooks that are a collection of the best recipes from the Junior Leagues throughout the Association.

Biscotti

2$\frac{1}{4}$ cups flour
$\frac{1}{2}$ cup cornmeal
1$\frac{1}{2}$ teaspoons baking powder
$\frac{1}{2}$ teaspoon salt
$\frac{1}{2}$ cup (1 stick) butter, softened

1 cup sugar
2 eggs
1 tablespoon anisette liqueur
1$\frac{1}{2}$ tablespoons anise seeds
1$\frac{1}{4}$ cups almonds

Mix the flour, cornmeal, baking powder and salt together. Beat the butter and sugar in a mixing bowl until light and fluffy. Add the eggs and beat well. Beat in the anisette liqueur, anise seeds and almonds. Add the flour mixture and mix well. Shape into 4 logs 2 inches wide. Place on a cookie sheet. Bake at 325 degrees for 35 minutes or until a light golden brown. Cool on the cookie sheet. Cut diagonally into pieces.

Makes about 2 dozen

Chocolate Mint Brownies

$\frac{1}{2}$ cup (1 stick) butter, softened
1 cup sugar
4 eggs, beaten
1 cup flour
$\frac{1}{2}$ teaspoon salt
1 teaspoon vanilla extract
1 (16-ounce) can chocolate syrup

2 cups confectioners' sugar
$\frac{1}{2}$ cup (1 stick) butter, softened
3 tablespoons crème de menthe
Green food coloring
6 tablespoons butter
1 cup (6 ounces) chocolate chips

Beat $\frac{1}{2}$ cup butter and sugar in a mixing bowl until light and fluffy. Add the eggs and beat well. Add the flour, salt, vanilla and chocolate syrup and mix well. Pour into a 9×13-inch baking pan sprayed lightly with nonstick cooking spray. Bake at 350 degrees for 30 minutes. Cool in the pan. Beat the confectioners' sugar, $\frac{1}{2}$ cup butter and crème de menthe in a mixing bowl until smooth. Add green food coloring 1 drop at a time until the desired tint is reached, blending well after each addition. Spread over the cooled brownies. Melt 6 tablespoons butter and chocolate chips in a saucepan over low heat, stirring constantly. Drizzle over the crème de menthe layer. Chill, covered, for 10 minutes or longer before cutting into bars.

Makes 2 dozen

Triple-Chocolate Brownies

1 1/2 cups flour
1/3 cup baking cocoa
1/2 teaspoon baking powder
1/4 teaspoon salt
8 ounces Snickers candy bars,
    cut into 1/4-inch pieces
2 cups sugar

4 eggs
3/4 cup (1 1/2 sticks) butter,
    melted, cooled
2 teaspoons vanilla extract
1/2 cup pecans, coarsely chopped
1 cup (6 ounces) milk chocolate
    chips

Mix the first 4 ingredients in a bowl. Place 1/4 cup of the flour mixture in a sealable plastic bag. Add the candy pieces. Seal the bag and shake to coat. Beat the sugar, eggs, butter and vanilla in a bowl until smooth. Add the remaining flour mixture and whisk for 50 strokes or until blended. Stir in the candy pieces and pecans. Spread in a 9×13-inch baking pan sprayed with nonstick cooking spray. Sprinkle the chocolate chips evenly over the top. Bake at 350 degrees for 30 minutes. Serve warm with vanilla ice cream or chill and cut into 2-inch squares.

Makes 2 dozen

Chocolate Caramel Layer Squares

1 (14-ounce) package caramels
1/3 cup evaporated milk
1 (2-layer) package German
    chocolate cake mix
1/3 cup evaporated milk

3/4 cup (1 1/2 sticks) butter,
    softened
1 cup pecans, chopped
1 cup (6 ounces) semisweet
    chocolate chips

Place the caramels in a double boiler. Add 1/3 cup evaporated milk. Cook over hot water until the caramels melt, stirring constantly. Combine the cake mix, 1/3 cup evaporated milk and butter in a mixing bowl and beat to form a soft dough. Stir in the pecans. Press 1/2 of the cake mixture into a greased 9×13-inch baking pan. Bake at 350 degrees for 6 minutes. Sprinkle with the chocolate chips, spreading evenly. Drizzle with the caramel mixture. Crumble the remaining cake mixture over the top. Bake for 15 to 18 minutes or until the edges pull from the sides of the pan. Let stand until cool. Chill, covered, for 30 minutes. Cut into squares.

Makes 2 dozen

From the Wine List

You've attended a wine class and assembled a modest little collection of your favorites. You want to introduce them to your friends, but you're afraid you don't have the right glassware. Don't worry, a simple clear glass works best for any wine-tasting. White wines are best suited to a smaller glass that tapers to the top, which helps keep it chilled. Larger glasses with a wide bottomed bowl are perfect for reds. Champagnes need tulip-shaped flutes that keep those tiny bubbles from escaping.

A simple clear glass works best for any wine-tasting.

Congo Squares

2³/4 cups flour
1¹/2 teaspoons baking powder
¹/2 teaspoon salt
1 (1-pound) package light brown
   sugar
²/3 cup shortening, melted, or
   vegetable oil

3 eggs
1 teaspoon lemon juice
¹/2 cup pecans, chopped
1 cup (6 ounces) chocolate chips

Sift the flour, baking powder and salt together. Combine the brown sugar and melted shortening in a large mixing bowl. Add the eggs 1 at a time, beating well after each addition. Add the flour mixture and lemon juice and mix well. Stir in the pecans and chocolate chips. Press into a lightly greased 9×13-inch baking pan. Bake at 350 degrees for 25 minutes. Let stand until cool. Cut into squares.

Makes 2 dozen

Coconut Macaroons

1 (14-ounce) package flaked
   coconut
1 (14-ounce) can sweetened
   condensed milk

1 teaspoon vanilla extract
1 teaspoon almond extract

Pulse the coconut in a food processor or blender a few times to break up any lumps or long strands. Combine the coconut, condensed milk and flavorings in a bowl and mix well. Drop by tablespoonfuls 1 inch apart on a cookie sheet lined with parchment paper. Bake at 325 degrees for 10 to 12 minutes or until light golden brown around the edges. Remove immediately to wire racks to cool.

Makes 4 dozen

Variation: For Chocolate Macaroons, add 4 ounces of melted semisweet chocolate to the batter or drizzle chocolate over the top after baking.

Coconut Bars

1 (2-layer) package yellow cake mix
1/2 cup (1 stick) margarine, melted
1 egg
1 cup pecans, chopped
1 to 1 1/2 cups shredded coconut
8 ounces cream cheese, softened
1 (1-pound) package confectioners' sugar
2 eggs
1 teaspoon vanilla extract

Combine the cake mix, margarine and 1 egg in a mixing bowl. Beat at medium speed until smooth. Press into a 9×13-inch glass baking dish sprayed lightly with nonstick cooking spray. Sprinkle with the pecans and coconut.

Beat the cream cheese, confectioners' sugar, 2 eggs and vanilla in a mixing bowl until smooth. Pour over the top. Bake at 350 degrees for 40 minutes. Remove from the oven and cool completely. Chill in the refrigerator before cutting into bars.

Makes 3 dozen

Variations on a Bar Cookie

These Coconut Bars are one of the most versatile desserts tested in our Junior League kitchens. Substitute German chocolate cake mix for the yellow cake mix in the recipe to add a continental flair. The youngster in your family (is that you?) will love it when you layer 6 ounces of semisweet or white chocolate chips over the coconut. Substitute macadamia nuts for the pecans and add an exotic layer to your treats. Do all of these substitutions and every chocoholic from miles around will come running to sample your delicious treats.

These Coconut Bars are one of the most versatile desserts tested in our Junior League kitchens.

Forgotten Meringue Cookies

2 egg whites
1 teaspoon vanilla extract
1/4 teaspoon cream of tartar
Pinch of salt

3/4 cup sugar
1 cup (6 ounces) chocolate chips
1/4 cup chopped nuts (optional)

Beat the egg whites, vanilla, cream of tartar and salt in a mixing bowl until soft peaks form. Add the sugar gradually, beating until stiff peaks form. Fold in the chocolate chips and nuts. Drop by teaspoonfuls onto cookie sheets lightly sprayed with nonstick cooking spray. Place in a 400-degree oven. Turn off the oven. Let stand in the oven for 8 to 12 hours. Do not open the oven door.

Makes 2 dozen

Note: You may take the cookies out of the oven sooner, but not before the oven has cooled completely.

Gingersnaps

2 cups flour
2 teaspoons baking soda
1/4 teaspoon salt
1 teaspoon cinnamon
1 teaspoon ground cloves
1 teaspoon ginger

3/4 cup butter-flavor shortening
1 cup sugar
1/4 cup molasses
1 egg
Sugar

Sift the flour, baking soda, salt, cinnamon, cloves and ginger together. Cream the shortening and 1 cup sugar in a mixing bowl. Add the molasses and egg and beat well. Add the flour mixture and mix well. Roll into small balls, adding additional flour if necessary to make the dough easy to handle. Dip in sugar and place 2 inches apart on lightly greased cookie sheets. Bake at 375 degrees for 10 to 12 minutes or until golden brown. Cool on wire racks.

Makes 250 to 300 small cookies

Note: These cookies will be about the size of a quarter. To make medium-size cookies, roll into larger-size balls and bake for 12 to 14 minutes.

Lemon Squares

2 cups flour
1 cup (2 sticks) butter, chilled, cut into small pieces
1/2 cup confectioners' sugar
1 teaspoon grated lemon zest
4 eggs
2 cups sugar
2 tablespoons grated lemon zest
1/3 cup fresh lemon juice
1/4 cup flour
1/2 teaspoon baking powder
1/2 cup sliced almonds
Confectioners' sugar

For the crust, process 2 cups flour, butter, 1/2 cup confectioners' sugar and 1 teaspoon lemon zest in a food processor to form a ball. Pat evenly into a lightly buttered 9×13-inch baking dish. Bake at 350 degrees for 20 to 25 minutes or until light brown. Remove from the oven to cool.

For the filling, process the eggs, sugar, 2 tablespoons lemon zest, lemon juice, 1/4 cup flour and baking powder in a food processor until smooth. Pour over the crust. Return to the oven. Bake for 25 minutes. Remove from the oven to cool. Sprinkle the almonds and confectioners' sugar over the cooled layer. Cut into 2-inch squares.

Makes 2 dozen

Holiday Fun that Helps Others

In 1997, the League expanded its annual holiday market for members and their friends to include families and the community. The Gingerbread Market features vendors offering a unique variety of gifts. Children are our special guests, with opportunities provided for them to make holiday gifts and crafts in the Children's Corner, enjoy a breakfast with Santa, or attend special storytelling events. Like our other fund-raisers, proceeds from this event go to support League projects.

Peanut Butter Toffee Cookies

1$\frac{1}{2}$ cups flour
1 teaspoon baking soda
$\frac{1}{8}$ teaspoon salt
$\frac{1}{2}$ cup shortening
$\frac{1}{2}$ cup packed brown sugar
$\frac{1}{2}$ cup sugar
1 egg, beaten
$\frac{1}{2}$ cup creamy peanut butter
1 teaspoon vanilla extract
8 ounces milk chocolate toffee bits

Mix the flour, baking soda and salt in a large bowl. Cream the shortening, brown sugar and sugar in a large mixing bowl until light and fluffy. Add the egg and beat well. Stir in the peanut butter and vanilla. Add the flour mixture gradually, stirring well after each addition. Stir in the toffee bits. Shape into small balls. Place 2 inches apart on nonstick cookie sheets. Bake at 375 degrees for 6 to 8 minutes. Remove to wire racks to cool.

Makes 3 dozen

Pecan Crescents

1 cup (2 sticks) butter or margarine, softened
3 tablespoons sugar
2 cups pecans, finely chopped
3 cups flour
1 teaspoon vanilla extract
Confectioners' sugar

Combine the butter, sugar, pecans, flour and vanilla in a mixing bowl and beat well. Shape the dough into 2-inch crescents. Place on ungreased cookie sheets. Bake at 250 degrees for 1 hour. Sprinkle the hot cookies with confectioners' sugar, turning gently to coat all sides. Cool on wire racks. Store in an airtight container.

Makes 4 dozen

Snickerdoodles

1/2 cup (1 stick) butter, softened
1/2 cup shortening
1 1/2 cups sugar
2 eggs
2 teaspoons vanilla extract
2 3/4 cups flour
2 teaspoons cream of tartar
1 teaspoon baking soda
1/4 teaspoon salt
2 tablespoons sugar
2 teaspoons cinnamon

Cream the butter, shortening and 1 1/2 cups sugar in a large mixing bowl until light and fluffy. Add the eggs and vanilla and mix well. Stir in the flour, cream of tartar, baking soda and salt. Shape the dough by rounded teaspoonfuls into balls. Mix 2 tablespoons sugar and cinnamon in a shallow bowl. Roll the balls in the cinnamon mixture to coat. Place 2 inches apart on ungreased cookie sheets. Bake at 400 degrees for 8 to 10 minutes or until set. Remove immediately to wire racks to cool.

Makes about 4 dozen

Special-K Cookies

1 cup white corn syrup
1 cup sugar
6 cups Special-K cereal
1 3/4 cups peanut butter
6 milk chocolate bars, melted

Heat the corn syrup and sugar in a saucepan over low heat until the sugar melts, stirring constantly. Remove from the heat. Let stand until cool enough to handle. Mix the cereal and peanut butter in a bowl. Add the warm syrup mixture and mix well by hand. Press into an 11×15-inch pan. Spread with the melted chocolate. Cool in the refrigerator. Cut into bars.

Makes 4 dozen

Tea Cookies

2 cups flour
1 teaspoon baking soda
1 teaspoon cream of tartar
1/2 cup (1 stick) butter, softened
1/4 cup vegetable oil
1 1/2 cups confectioners' sugar
1 egg
1 teaspoon vanilla extract

Mix the flour, baking soda and cream of tartar together. Combine the butter, oil, confectioners' sugar and egg in a mixing bowl and mix well. Add the flour mixture and stir until blended. Stir in the vanilla. Chill for 1 hour or longer. Shape the dough into 1-inch balls. Place 2 inches apart on ungreased cookie sheets. Bake at 350 degrees for 10 to 12 minutes or until golden brown. Remove to wire racks to cool.

Makes 30 cookies

Toffee Diamonds

1 cup (2 sticks) butter, softened
1 cup packed brown sugar
1 teaspoon vanilla extract
2 cups flour
3/4 cup chocolate chips
1 cup walnuts, chopped
Chocolate frosting
Walnut halves

Cream the butter, brown sugar and vanilla in a large mixing bowl until light and fluffy. Add the flour and mix well. Stir in the chocolate chips and chopped walnuts. Press into an ungreased 10×15-inch baking pan. Bake at 350 degrees for 25 minutes or until brown. Cut immediately into 2-inch diamond shapes. Let stand until cool. Remove from the pan. Dot each cookie with chocolate frosting. Arrange 1 walnut half on the top of each.

Makes 2 dozen

Urban Legend Cookies

2½ cups rolled oats
2 cups flour
1 teaspoon baking powder
1 teaspoon baking soda
½ teaspoon salt
1 cup (2 sticks) butter or margarine, softened
1 cup sugar
1 cup packed brown sugar
2 eggs
1 teaspoon vanilla extract
2 cups (12 ounces) semisweet chocolate chips
4 ounces premium milk chocolate, grated
1½ cups pecans, finely chopped

Process the oats in a food processor or blender to form a fine powder. Mix the processed oats, flour, baking powder, baking soda and salt in a large bowl.

Cream the butter, sugar and brown sugar in a large mixing bowl until light and fluffy. Add the eggs 1 at a time, beating well after each addition. Add the vanilla and mix well. Stir in the flour mixture. Add the chocolate chips, milk chocolate and pecans and stir to mix well.

Drop the dough by rounded teaspoonfuls onto ungreased cookie sheets. Bake at 375 degrees for 6 to 8 minutes or until golden brown. Remove to wire racks to cool.

Makes about 5 dozen

Preserving an Heirloom

One of the pleasures of a handed-down recipe is the paper it's actually printed on. Whether it's on intricate stationery or handwritten by a beloved grandmother, no amount of stains or rips will make your family's recipe less precious. Your kids will find it a comforting record of family memories, recalling the tastes and aromas of mom's cooking when they go off to college or get married. For a special gift, collect these treasured recipes and have them mounted in a special frame. It's a sweet personal accent for anyone's kitchen.

For a special gift, collect these treasured recipes and have them mounted in a special frame.

Sour Cream Apple Pie

2 tablespoons flour
3/4 cup sugar
1/4 teaspoon salt
1/4 teaspoon nutmeg
1 egg, beaten
1 cup sour cream
1 teaspoon vanilla extract
3 cups chopped peeled apples
1 unbaked (9-inch) pie shell
Cinnamon Topping (below)

Mix the flour, sugar, salt and nutmeg in a large bowl. Combine the egg, sour cream and vanilla in a small bowl and mix well. Add to the flour mixture and mix well. Stir in the apples. Spoon into the pie shell. Bake at 400 degrees for 15 minutes. Reduce the oven temperature to 350 degrees. Bake for 30 minutes longer. Remove from the oven. Increase the oven temperature to 400 degrees. Sprinkle Cinnamon Topping over the pie. Return to the oven. Bake for 10 minutes. Remove to a wire rack to cool.

Serves 8

Cinnamon Topping

1/3 cup sugar
1/3 cup flour
1 teaspoon cinnamon
2 tablespoons butter

Combine the sugar, flour and cinnamon in a small bowl. Cut in the butter until crumbly.

Makes 2/3 cup

Chocolate Chip Pecan Pie

1 unbaked (9-inch) pie shell
2 eggs
1/2 cup flour
1/2 cup sugar
1/2 cup packed brown sugar
1/4 cup (1/2 stick) butter, melted, cooled
1 cup (6 ounces) semisweet chocolate chips
1 cup pecans, chopped

Pierce the pie shell several times with a fork. Bake at 325 degrees for 8 minutes. Remove from the oven. Beat the eggs in a large mixing bowl until foamy. Add the flour, sugar and brown sugar and beat well. Stir in the butter, chocolate chips and pecans. Pour into the prebaked pie shell. Bake for 1 hour. Remove from the oven and cool for 30 minutes. Serve warm with ice cream.

Serves 8

Chocolate Crunch Pie

1/3 cup margarine
1 cup (6 ounces) semisweet chocolate chips
2 1/2 cups crisp rice cereal
1 pint ice cream
Ice cream toppings

Melt the margarine and chocolate chips in a heavy saucepan over low heat. Remove from the heat. Stir in the cereal until completely coated. Press over the bottom and up the side of a buttered 10-inch deep-dish pie plate. Chill, covered, for 30 minutes. Fill with your favorite ice cream. Drizzle with your favorite ice cream toppings.

Serves 8

Note: Try such combinations as chocolate chip ice cream drizzled with crème de menthe and chocolate fudge sauce. Or, try butter pecan ice cream drizzled with caramel sauce and chocolate syrup.

Chocolate Meringue Pie

1 cup sugar
1/3 cup flour
6 tablespoons baking cocoa
1/2 teaspoon salt
2 1/2 cups milk
3 egg yolks
2 tablespoons butter
2 teaspoons vanilla extract
1 baked (9-inch) pie shell
3 egg whites
1 teaspoon vanilla extract
1/2 teaspoon cream of tartar

Mix the sugar, flour, baking cocoa and salt in a bowl. Scald the milk in a saucepan. Pour 1/2 cup of the scalded milk into a bowl. Let stand until cool. Add the sugar mixture to the remaining milk in the saucepan. Cook over medium heat until thickened, stirring constantly.

Mix the cool milk with the egg yolks. Add to the chocolate mixture gradually, stirring constantly. Cook for 3 minutes, stirring constantly. Remove from the heat. Add the butter and 2 teaspoons vanilla. Cool slightly. Pour into the baked pie shell.

Beat the egg whites, 1 teaspoon vanilla and cream of tartar in a mixing bowl until stiff peaks form. Spread over the chocolate filling. Bake at 350 degrees for 15 minutes.

Serves 8

Nanny's Coconut Cream Pie

3/4 cup sugar
1/4 cup cornstarch
1/4 teaspoon salt
2 cups milk
3 egg yolks
2 tablespoons butter
1 teaspoon vanilla extract
1 cup flaked coconut
1 baked (9-inch) pie shell
1 cup whipping cream
1/4 cup sifted confectioners' sugar
2 tablespoons flaked coconut, toasted

Combine 3/4 cup sugar, cornstarch and salt in a heavy saucepan. Stir in the milk gradually. Cook over medium heat until thickened and bubbly, stirring constantly. Cook for 1 minute longer. Beat the egg yolks in a small bowl. Stir about 1/4 of the hot mixture gradually into the egg yolks. Add to the remaining hot mixture. Cook for 30 seconds, stirring constantly. Remove from the heat. Stir in the butter, vanilla and 1 cup coconut. Pour into the baked pie shell. Cool completely. Chill, covered, for 1 to 2 hours.

Beat the whipping cream at high speed in a mixing bowl until foamy. Add the confectioners' sugar 1 tablespoon at a time, beating constantly until stiff peaks form. Pipe or dollop onto the pie. Sprinkle with the toasted coconut.

Serves 8

Pie-in-the-Sky Perfection

What's the secret to a delicious crust? Lots of patience and a few tips from our Junior League kitchens:

* *For the richest color and flavor, use whole milk and butter-flavor shortening.*
* *Use all-purpose flour, not cake flour.*
* *For a lighter color and a mellow flavor, use ice water and plain shortening.*
* *The colder the water, the flakier the crust will be.*
* *A pastry blender is a great tool for cutting in fat, but two knives will get you the same results.*
* *Use a fork to mix dough as water is added so your hands won't soften the shortening too much.*
* *Glass pie dishes make a darker crust than aluminum ones.*

Lemonade Pies

1 (14-ounce) can sweetened condensed milk
1 (6-ounce) can frozen lemonade or limeade concentrate, thawed
12 ounces whipped topping
Yellow or green food coloring (optional)
2 (9-inch) graham cracker or shortbread shells

Combine the condensed milk and lemonade concentrate in a bowl and mix well. Fold in the whipped topping. Tint with food coloring. Spoon into the pie shells. Chill, covered, for 8 to 12 hours.

Makes 2 pies

Note: For a more elegant presentation, spoon the filling into 12 tart shells. Top with whipped cream. Garnish with lemon or lime slices or a fresh strawberry.

Pecan Pie

$1/2$ cup sugar
2 tablespoons butter, softened
2 eggs, beaten
2 tablespoons flour
$1/4$ teaspoon salt
1 teaspoon almond extract
1 cup white corn syrup
$1^1/2$ cups pecans, chopped
1 unbaked (9-inch) pie shell

Cream the sugar and butter in a mixing bowl until light and fluffy. Add the eggs, flour, salt, almond extract and corn syrup and stir until blended. Fold in the pecans. Pour into the pie shell. Bake at 350 degrees for 30 minutes or until a knife inserted in the center comes out clean.

Serves 8

Praline Pumpkin Pies

2 cups pecans, finely chopped
1 cup packed brown sugar
1 cup (2 sticks) margarine, melted
2 teaspoons cinnamon
3 unbaked (10-inch) deep-dish
   pie shells
4 eggs, lightly beaten
1 (30-ounce) can solid-pack
   pumpkin

1¹/₂ cups sugar
1 teaspoon salt
1 teaspoon cinnamon
1 teaspoon ginger
¹/₂ teaspoon cloves
2 (12-ounce) cans evaporated
   milk

Mix the pecans, brown sugar, margarine and 2 teaspoons cinnamon in a small bowl. Spread evenly in the pie shells. Combine the eggs, pumpkin, sugar, salt, 1 teaspoon cinnamon, ginger, cloves and evaporated milk in the order listed in a large bowl and mix well. Pour over the praline mixture in the pie shells. Bake at 425 degrees for 15 minutes. Reduce the oven temperature to 350 degrees. Bake for 45 minutes longer or until a knife inserted in the center comes out clean. Cool on wire racks.

Makes 3 pies

Pecan Tarts

3 ounces cream cheese, softened
6 tablespoons butter, softened
1 cup flour
1 egg, beaten

2 tablespoons butter, melted
³/₄ cup packed brown sugar
¹/₂ cup chopped pecans

Mix the cream cheese, 6 tablespoons butter and flour in a bowl to form a soft dough. Shape into 24 small balls. Place each ball in a miniature muffin cup sprayed lightly with nonstick cooking spray, shaping the dough to line each cup. Combine the egg, 2 tablespoons butter, brown sugar and pecans in a bowl and mix well. Spoon into each pastry-lined cup. Bake at 350 degrees for 30 minutes.

Makes 2 dozen

Coffee—the Grand Finale

With the variety of available blends greater than ever before, the choices for an after-dinner cup of coffee are more complex than just "decaf" or "regular." And with inexpensive coffee bean grinders flooding the market, it's easier than ever to get a fresh-brewed cup right in your own kitchen. In our last chapter, you'll find great ideas for an easy dessert and coffee buffet party that fits into any budget or entertaining space. Let this Irish Coffee recipe spark your coffee creativity!

Classic Irish Coffee

1 teaspoon sugar
2 tablespoons Irish
   whiskey
²/₃ cup hot coffee
¹/₄ cup whipping
   cream, whipped

Place the sugar and whiskey in a glass coffee mug. Stir in the coffee. Top with the whipped cream.

Alpharetta

What started as a tiny tent village with one log schoolhouse has evolved into a sprawling township with seemingly a school on every corner. Alpharetta's name was derived from the Greek words for first (ALPHA) and town (RETTA). As the county seat for what was once Milton County, Alpharetta experienced its first boom as a center for cotton farming. Now it is the center of the explosion of white-collar business and technology in northern Fulton County.

Civic pride runs strong in Alpharetta. There are parades through the town square on Old Soldiers' Day, and horse shows at Wills Park Equestrian Center. Volunteer opportunities include the Alpharetta Clean and Beautiful environmental campaign, the Alpharetta Historical Society, and various other services for senior citizens, the arts, and schools.

Alpharettans stretch their bodies and their minds through the variety of programs from the Parks and Recreation Department. Lots of picnicking and boating goes on along the Chattahoochee River as it winds its way through Alpharetta. Trails in the Big Creek area near North Point Mall ensure that everyone has access to the natural beauty and charm of the Alpharetta area.

At Your Service

Menus and Serving Ideas

Courtside Cuisine

Service for 20

Smoked Oyster Dip with
pita chips, crackers and fresh vegetables
Page 21

Greek Pasta Salad
Page 77

Fruit Kabobs with Yogurt Sauce
Page 167

Pesto Pinwheels
Page 22

Pizza Bread
Page 92

Lemon Squares
Page 153

Triple-Chocolate Brownies
Page 149

Spiced Iced Tea
Page 26

In tennis-crazy Gwinnett and North Fulton counties, the food at the matches takes center court. During a round robin, this menu will feed five matches full of hungry doubles players. Use these tips for a smashing presentation!

- ❖ To prepare Fruit Kabobs, thread alternate chunks of fruit onto short wooden skewers. For Yogurt Sauce for dipping, mix one carton of vanilla yogurt with one small carton of sour cream.

- ❖ Stick fruit kabobs into a whole pineapple for a yummy centerpiece.

- ❖ Use cake plates of differing heights to make the table interesting and easier to access. Stack the desserts alternately on tiered plates for a colorful presentation.

- ❖ To keep beverages cold, line a gym bag with a heavy-duty plastic bag and dump in the ice and cold ones. What could be more appropriate (or portable) for a tennis match?

- ❖ Cover a racquet head with plastic wrap and serve the Pizza Bread on it.

If your team wins the city championships (or you need to drown your sorrows), pop open a sparkling Champagne "look-alike" such as Nino Franco's "Rustico." Its fresh, fruity taste and effervescence complements the menu here.

Tailgate Party for Sports Nuts

Service for 16

Mexican Caviar with tortilla chips
Page 16

Jalapeño Cheese Bites
Page 25

"Dig Deep" Salad
Page 66

Caraway Breadsticks
Page 40

Smoked Sesame Tenderloin
Page 88

Chocolate Chip Cake
Page 139

Bourbon Slush
Page 26

Whether it's a college football game or your child's soccer tournament, picnicking in the parking lot is a time-honored tradition in sports. Invite your alumni buddies to join you, for this menu will feed up to sixteen people. These recipes were selected for their portability and ease in serving—the pork tenderloin tastes just as good cold as it does warmed.

❖ Decorating with your team colors is a given. Use a school flag or stadium blanket with the appropriate colors as a cover for that folding table.

❖ Chairs that telescope up into a slender tote bag are inexpensive, easy to find, and ideal for outdoor seating.

❖ Fill one picnic basket with all of the table setting items. Set this on top of everything else so you can access it quickly.

❖ Be sure to fill a cooler with water bottles, soft drinks, and beer. Use regional breweries for a taste of the best local flavors. In the Gwinnett and North Fulton area, try brews by Sweetwater, Atlanta Brewing Company, and Dogwood Brewing Company.

❖ Don't forget a bag filled with these essentials: plastic garbage bags, wet wipes, a gallon of water, a corkscrew and bottle opener, and a battery-powered radio to listen to the pre-game show.

First-Ever Supper Club Dinner

Service for 6

Sausage-Stuffed Mushrooms
WINE SUGGESTION: French White Sancerre

Page 25

Crisp Mixed Greens with Apple and Warm Brie
Page 67

Rosemary-Crusted Roasted Lamb
WINE SUGGESTION: Chateâuneuf-du-Pape

Page 87

Three-Cheese Mashed Potatoes
Page 115

Glazed Carrots
Page 109

Curried Fruit
Page 123

Chocolate Toffee Trifle
WINE SUGGESTION: Banyuls

Page 135

Have you ever wanted to start a supper club? There are lots of good reasons to get one going. Maybe you have friends scattered all over the area that need to schedule get-togethers far in advance. Or there are new neighbors you'd like to know better. Or maybe you just like to eat? Start your first meeting with a menu as simple as this one and some tips from experienced supper clubbers:

❖ Plan to meet every other month and set a consistent date— say, the third Saturday night.

❖ Elect one member "King" or "Queen" and have that person set up a rotating schedule for one year. Send out the schedule for gatherings as soon as it's finalized.

❖ The hosts will be responsible for selecting the menu and preparing the entrée. They should send recipes out with the invitations so everyone will know specifically what to bring.

❖ A theme isn't necessary, but it's fun. Find ideas at party and stationery stores. Floral notepaper can inspire a garden party, or leis might lead you to a luau.

❖ An experienced wine retailer can help you tailor your wine selection for every course. For this menu, the Sancerre is a wine made with the Sauvignon Blanc grape that is dry, crisp, and very clean. Chateâuneuf-du-Pape is a full-bodied red wine that complements the lamb beautifully, and the Banyuls is a sweet French fortified wine perfect for a chocolate dessert.

Ladies' Brunch in the Garden

Service for 8

BLT Bites
Page 23

Fruit Salsa with Cinnamon Sugar Chips
Page 19

Cheese Straws
Page 24

Napa Salad with chopped cooked chicken
Page 71

Orange Muffins
Page 42

Cream Cheese Pound Cake
served à la mode
Page 141

This menu lends itself to an outdoor, garden setting. It's ideal if you're having a party with a guest of honor, like a bridal or baby shower, or for the birthday of an older relative. If you prefer, serve the Napa Salad with shrimp instead of chicken. Set up a selection of toppings for the pound cake, such as chocolate syrup, strawberries, or chopped cookie bits.

❖ Greet each guest with a flute of Champagne with a floating strawberry garnish. Try Taittinger or Moet & Chandon's "White Star." A California Chardonnay would also be perfect for this menu.

❖ Make the guest of honor feel special with a corsage.

❖ Take instant pictures as the guests arrive. Take one with everyone at the party and use it as the centerpiece of a collage that you can frame and present to your special guest.

❖ Framing the invitation or the menu and placing on the table is a nice touch.

❖ Use scarves as a tablecloth for an airy, colorful touch.

❖ Provide a large, handled shopping bag in which the guest of honor can take her gifts home.

New Southern Sunday Supper

Service for 12

Hot Artichoke Dip
Page 12

Slow-Cooked Pot Roast
Page 85

Green Bean Bundles
Page 111

Squash Soufflé
Page 117

Angel Biscuits
Page 33

Quick and Easy Banana Pudding
Page 130

Iced Tea

Introduce new friends to the flavors of the South. This menu begins with a hearty appetizer and fills up everyone through every course, all the way through to dessert. If your family's not in town, invite the neighbors over for a good old-fashioned get-together. Tell everyone to wear expandable-waist pants!

❖ This menu would work well for a day filled with watching football on TV. Serve this supper around 2 or 3 P.M.—that should be around halftime!

❖ If your guests are not native southerners, odds are they're probably confused about the term "supper." Explain that "dinner" in the South is the midday meal (or Sunday lunch). "Supper" is what's left over from "dinner"!

❖ For a true southern experience, omit the meat entrée and add one or two more vegetable side dishes for a true "home cooking" experience. Try adding the Home-Syle Macaroni and Cheese, Southern Corn Bread Dressing, or Sweet Potato Soufflé from our Side Dishes chapter.

❖ Add a down-home touch with a red-checked tablecloth and stoneware servers. Set beverages out in a big galvanized steel tub full of ice.

❖ If weather permits, serve this meal outside on a big screened porch.

Holiday Dessert Buffet

Service for 10

Coconut Bars
Page 151

Chocolate Mint Brownies
Page 148

Piña Colada Cheesecake
Page 128

Pecan Tarts
Page 163

Coffee Charlotte
Page 133

Biscotti
Page 148

Red Velvet Cake
Page 142

Chocolate Bourbon Truffles
Page 146

Coffee Bar
Page 177

This festive menu makes a beautiful presentation with its array of colors, textures, and shapes. To make your buffet table sparkle, use your finest silver and crystal serving pieces, dessert plates, and lots of flickering candles. To top the night off, set up a coffee bar. This is an easy way to entertain your friends during the busy holiday season.

Setting up a coffee bar:

❖ Dessert blends are available at specialty coffeehouses or your local farmer's market. Try Chocolate, Cookies N' Cream, Raspberry, Amaretto, and Vanilla Cream.

❖ If some guests are skipping dessert and want a rich coffee, try White Chocolate Mousse, Hazelnut, Tiramisu, or Irish Cream. It's a guilt-free pleasure at only eight calories on average and zero grams of fat!

❖ Set out the necessary garnishes of cream and sugar, and add allspice, cinnamon vanilla, cocoa, and nutmeg. Offer cinnamon sticks or reception sticks for stirring.

❖ Let guests create their own gourmet coffee drinks. Set out a selection of rum, whiskey, and specialty liqueurs. The most popular flavors are coffee, orange, hazelnut, cream, brandy, and Cognac.

Quick-Fix Appetizers

With 8 ounces cream cheese:

❖ Shape the softened cream cheese as desired. Pour jalapeño or red pepper jelly over the cream cheese. Garnish and serve with assorted crackers. Try minced green onions as a garnish over red pepper jelly.

❖ Mix the softened cream cheese with 1 small can deviled ham and 1 garlic clove, minced. Serve with mini-bagels.

❖ Add 4 ounces of feta cheese, 2 tablespoons chopped fresh basil and 2 tablespoons chopped sun-dried tomatoes to the softened cream cheese and mix well. Serve with Italian bread.

❖ Add 1 small jar of pasteurized cheese product to the softened cream cheese and mix well. Stir in minced green onions. Serve with an assortment of vegetables.

❖ Microwave the cream cheese on High for 15 to 20 seconds or until softened. Stir in your favorite herbs. Serve with crackers.

❖ Soften the cream cheese and mix with 8 ounces sour cream, $1/3$ cup packed brown sugar and $1/4$ teaspoon ground cinnamon. Serve with fruit.

With 1 cup of sour cream:

❖ Add a 10-ounce package of frozen chopped spinach, thawed and drained; 1 can water chestnuts, drained, chopped; and your favorite spices; chill. Serve with assorted crackers.

❖ Mix with 1 envelope French onion dip or soup mix. Serve with vegetables.

❖ For an easy shrimp dip, combine the sour cream, 3 ounces softened cream cheese, 1 envelope Italian salad dressing mix, 1 can of tiny shrimp, chopped, and 2 teaspoons lemon juice.

❖ Mix with $1/2$ cup ranch salad dressing, $1/4$ cup grated Parmesan cheese, crumbled cooked bacon and green onion slices; chill. Serve with vegetables or crackers.

❖ For an easy Mexican dip, increase the sour cream to 2 cups and stir in 1 envelope ranch salad dressing mix and $1/2$ cup salsa; chill. Serve with tortilla chips.

Save yourself time and stress by taking advantage of ready-made items in your local supermarket.

❖ Hummus served with whole baby carrots or pita crisps

❖ Spiced or salted nuts

❖ Antipasto tray—marinated olives, artichokes, cherry or grape tomatoes, and cubed mozzarella

❖ Gourmet cheese assortment

❖ Frozen hors d'oeuvre

❖ Pinwheel sandwiches from the deli

❖ Ready-made sushi with soy sauce or hot mustard

What's for Dinner?

Ever find yourself standing in front of the refrigerator or pantry waiting for a dinner idea to jump out at you? Keeping these main ingredients handy will make that job easier. Here are a few of our favorites.

With a pound or two of ground beef:
❖ Chili Cheese Dip, page 14
❖ Taco Salad, page 75
❖ Chuckwagon Beans, page 108
❖ Cowboy Stew, page 60
❖ Park Ranger Jerry's Chili, page 63
❖ Garden Beef and Rice, page 87
❖ Old-Fashioned Meat Loaf, page 86

With a pound of ground sausage:
❖ Sausage-Stuffed Mushrooms, page 25
❖ Apple Sausage Quiche, page 48
❖ Breakfast Casserole, page 48
❖ Corn Bread Shrimp Supreme, page 101
❖ St. Paul's Rice, page 122

With leftover holiday ham:
❖ Breakfast Casserole, page 48
❖ Ham and Cheese Rolls, page 47
❖ Ham and Asparagus Brunch Bake, page 47
❖ Hoppin' John, page 113

With 2 cups chopped, cooked chicken:
❖ Tortilla Soup, page 58
❖ Southwest White Chili, page 62
❖ Chicken Packets, page 93
❖ Hot Chicken Salad, page 96
❖ Creamy Chicken Enchiladas, page 92
❖ Chicken Tetrazzini, page 98

A Wine Glossary

Acidity—how sharp, or tart, the wine tastes.

Aroma—the smell of the grapes in the wine.

Beaujolais—a light, fruity, red Burgundy wine from the region of the same name in France.

Blanc de Blancs—White wine made from white grapes.

Blanc de Noir—White wine made from red grapes.

Bouquet—the smell of the wine itself.

Brut—a dry style of Champagne.

Bordeaux—an important wine-producing region in France known primarily for red wines.

Burgundy—a wine-producing region in France whose name has become synonymous with red wines.

Cabernet Sauvignon—a red grape grown in France and California.

Chablis—a white wine made with chardonnay grapes grown in the Chablis district.

Champagne—the region in France that produces the sparkling wine known as Champagne.

Chardonnay—a white grape grown all over the world.

Chenin Blanc—a white grape grown in the Loire Valley of France and California.

Chianti—a red wine from the Tuscany region of Italy.

Cuvee—an especially prepared blend of wine.

Decant—to pour wine gently from the bottle into a carafe to separate the sediment in the bottle.

Dry—the opposite of sweet; free of sugar.

Estate-bottled—wine made, produced, and bottled by the vineyard's owner.

Fruity—having the fragrance of a familiar fruit, like blackberry.

Gewürztraminer—A "spicy" white grape grown in Alsace, France, California, and Germany.

Merlot—the "softer" red grape grown primarily in France, California, and Chile.

Mellow—wine that is soft in taste.

Nose—the term used for describing the bouquet and aroma of wine.

Pinots—a family of grape varieties grown all over the world. Variations are Pinot Blanc, a common white varietal; Pinot Grigio, a white varietal with a full-bodied taste; and Pinot Noir, a red grape with a deep, distinctive taste.

Riesling—a white grape grown in Alsace, France, Germany, and California.

Sauvignon Blanc—a white grape grown in France and California, sometimes called Fume Blanc.

Sour—indicates a wine that has spoiled. Not to be used instead of "tart."

Syrah—a red grape from France, also known as "Shiraz."

Tart—possessing fruity, pleasing acid tastes.

Varietal—the variety of grape from which the wine is made.

Vin blanc—white wine.

Vin rose—rose wine.

Vin rouge—red wine.

Vintage—the gathering of grapes and their fermentation into wine; also, the crop of grapes or wine of one season.

Zinfandel—a red grape grown in California with a fruity or berry flavor.

The Well-Stocked Pantry

Whether you are planning an intimate party or a week's worth of menus, a complete grocery list is key. If you are using *At Your Service* as a guide to menu planning, we've put together some items commonly used in our recipes. Keep these staples handy when making your grocery list and you'll never run out of ideas.

Refrigerator/Freezer:

Eggs
Whipping cream
Half-and-half
Milk
Cream cheese
Sour cream
Cheddar cheese
Parmesan cheese
Swiss cheese
Whipped topping

Refrigerated pie crusts
Refrigerated crescent rolls
Refrigerated biscuits
Butter/margarine
Orange juice
Lemons
Celery
Salad greens
Mushrooms
Green onions

Spinach
Broccoli
Carrots
Yellow Squash
Bacon
Ground beef
Ground sausage
Chicken breasts
Pork tenderloin
Parsley

Pantry:

Variety of pasta
Rice
New red potatoes
White potatoes
Grits
Variety of soups
Variety of beans
Variety of corn
Chicken broth
Beef broth
Tomato sauce
Diced tomatoes
Soy sauce
Hot sauce
Vegetable/olive oil
Cider vinegar
Salsa
Mustard (yellow and Dijon)
Mayonnaise/salad dressing

Onions
Garlic
Baking soda
Baking powder
All-purpose flour
Salt
Pepper
Paprika
Dried basil
Cinnamon
Brown sugar
Sugar
Sweetened condensed milk
Evaporated milk
Light corn syrup
Nutmeg
Vanilla extract
Almond extract
Cajun seasonings

Pecans
Sliced almonds
Confectioners' sugar
Variety of chips
Variety of crackers
Variety of cake mixes
Instant puddings
Brownie mix
Baking cocoa
Chocolate chips
Bread crumbs
Quick-cooking oats
Stuffing mix
Canned shrimp
Canned crab meat
Raisins
Bananas
Apples
Peanut butter

Buffet Service

Buffet service is a must when space is limited. Here are a few guidelines to insure your party has a smooth traffic flow around the table:

❖ Start with the silverware, plates, and napkins. The entrée comes next, with side dishes and bread following. If room permits, set beverages and desserts on a separate table. If not, they should follow bread.

❖ Place serving pieces next to serving dishes.

❖ Roll the fork, knife, and spoon in a napkin and secure with a ribbon or ring.

❖ For a large crowd, use a rectangular table and serve down both sides.

❖ Use warming trays and chilled platters to keep food at the proper temperature.

❖ Avoid serving food that needs to be cut or has messy gravies and dressings.

❖ Couples should go through the line together—buffets are the exception to the rule, Ladies First.

Cookies Anyone?

Chocolate chip, gingersnap, peanut butter . . .who can decide? Take a few of each. Plan a cookie swap before the Christmas holidays or even Valentine's Day. Cookie swaps are an easy way to bring friends together for a little holiday cheer without devoting hours to preparation. Here are some tips to help make your cookie swap a mouth-watering success:

❖ Send out invitations, asking attendees to bring a batch or two of their cookies in a decorative tin, basket, or holiday platter and enough copies of their recipes for each guest. You may ask each guest to bring a container for carrying the cookies home or you may provide your guests with bags or baskets decorated for the season. Don't forget plenty of sealable plastic food storage bags to keep everyone's cookies fresh.

❖ Encourage guests to wear festive holiday attire. A set of copper or antique cookie cutters tied with ribbon makes a great door prize for the best outfit.

❖ Offer your guests an assortment of beverages, such as coffee, tea, and hot apple cider. A few non-sweet snacks, like our yummy Cheese Straws, give guests a chance to cleanse their palates between sampling all those sweet treats.

❖ Yes, bar cookies count! See our Desserts chapter for our favorites.

Contributor's List

League Members:
Meg Anderson
Jill Awbrey
Barbara Baker
JoAnn Barber
Tracy Bauer
Mary Beem
Jill Bernhardt
Mary Bierbusse
Nancy Blincoe
Rachel Bronnum
Susan Buck
Molly Burke
Susan Burks
Beth Burns
Teri Butler
Kris Carter
Julie Clark
Mary Ellen Cleveland
Heather Coble
Dixie Culver
Stephanie deJarnette
Jo Dills
Cindy Ehmer
Shana Elliott
Pam Elmore
Christine Fisher
Jane Freeman
Sandy Futch
Tracey Hill
Carole Hoemeke
Jennifer Hoff
Jennifer Horton
Jan Hughes
Noreen Jamison
Dottie Johnson
Susan Kendrick-Lauhoff
Eileen Lotz
Jill Lovett
Theresa Lucas
Penny Ann Machemehl
Kathy Malerstein

Patty Mallicote
Julia Marshall
Maureen Martin
Angela Meyer
Melissa Moon
Skylar Moss
Amy Nicola
Stephanie Owens
Mary Anne Payne
Pam Plaugher
Page Poer
Sharon Powell
Kerri Ray
Nanette Reilly
Susan Rickson
Macy Roush
Jacqueline Sandiford
Leslie Scarpa
LeRey Schrampher
Mary Stern
Cindy Sullivan
Stirling Sullivan
Anna Butters Tanner
Elizabeth Taylor
Cam McClellan Teems
Heather Trainor
Mary Stewart Trogdon
Summer Tucker
Nancy Van Patten
Betsy Wade
Dee Waters
Christa Watson
Heather Welch
Jo Alice Welton
Alison Wenz
Cindy Westmoreland
Jill Kirkpatrick Willis
Sandy Willyerd
Kris Wilson
Martha Wilson
Keyna Wintjen
Rebecca Woodcock

Peggy Woods
Karen Zambetti
Terri Zerbe

Friends of the League:
Martha Ann Allen
Lisa Aloia
Kathryn Arnold
Ruth Ann Blackwell
Karen Boyd
Carol Caldwell
Michelle Caricofe
Kristin Cottle
Brian DeBold
Jan Dymond
Roxanna Erwin
Miranda Faulkner
James and Kim Fowler
Meg Gay
Dana Grailer
Colleen Hicks
Judy, Jessica and
    Lindsay Hicks
Jerry Hightower
Lisa Holsonback
Heather Riggs Horton
Peggy Horton
Cathy Johnson
Debbi Makarenko
Ethel McKee
Hillary Pioso
Kathi Redfield
Pamela Reeves
Kelli Smith
Janet Stensgard
Tina Stevens
Lora Thompson
Tim and Ellen Thornton
Fred Van Patten
Rebecca Webb

Index

At Your Service

Southern Recipes, Places and Traditions

Junior League of Gwinnett and North Fulton Counties, Inc.
Cookbook Committee
3578 West Lawrenceville Street
Duluth, Georgia 30096
www.jlgnf.org
770-476-3090 • Fax: 770-392-0203

Name _____

Street Address _____

City _____ State _____ Zip _____

Telephone _____

YOUR ORDER	QTY	TOTAL
At Your Service at $19.95 per book		$
Postage and handling at $6.00 for first book; $1.00 for each additional book		$
Georgia residents add 6% sales tax		$
TOTAL		$

Method of Payment: [   ] MasterCard   [   ] VISA
[   ] Check enclosed payable to JLGNF

Credit Card Number _____ Expiration Date _____

Authorized Signature _____

Photocopies will be accepted.